MY UNCLE CHARLIE

JULIE SHAW

MY UNCLE CHARLIE

THE TRUE STORY OF YORKSHIRE'S NOTORIOUS CRIMINAL FAMILY

All names and identities have been changed in this memoir, to protect both
the living and the children of those who have died. Some changes have
been made to historical facts for the same reason.

HarperElement
An imprint of HarperCollins*Publishers*
77–85 Fulham Palace Road,
Hammersmith, London W6 8JB

www.harpercollins.co.uk

and HarperElement are trademarks of
HarperCollins*Publishers* Ltd

First published by HarperElement 2014

3 5 7 9 10 8 6 4 2

© Julie Shaw and Lynne Barrett-Lee 2014

Julie Shaw and Lynne Barrett-Lee assert the moral right
to be identified as the authors of this work

A catalogue record of this book is
available from the British Library

PB ISBN: 978-0-00-754226-0
EB ISBN: 978-0-00-754227-7

Printed and bound in Great Britain by
Clays Ltd, St Ives plc

Find out more about HarperCollins and the environment at
www.harpercollins.co.uk/green

The Final Countdown

Slouched, you slowly shuffle, unsure where
you'll safely sleep,
Hood hitched close, hiding your head as you
falter down High Street,
Weather beaten face and weary eyes, no longer
a welter weight,
A punch bag, a punk, a parasite now, you care
not to ponder your fate.

The bottle, the bag, the boxing brochure, bound
tightly beneath your belt,
The past, the present, the pain to come, no
prickle of pride to be felt,
A doorway, a dumpster to bed down in,
destined to die in the damp,
A chorus of chants cloud your chemical brain,
seconds out for the champ.

Note by the Author

My name is Julie Shaw, and my father, Keith, is the only surviving member of the 13 Hudson siblings, born to Annie and Reggie Hudson on the infamous Canterbury Estate in Bradford. We were and are a very close family, even though there were so many of us, and those of us who are left always will be.

I wanted to write these stories as a tribute to my parents and family. The stories are all based on the truth but, as I'm sure you'll understand, I've had to disguise some identities and facts to protect the innocent. Those of you who still live on the Canterbury Estate will appreciate the folklore that we all grew up with: the stories of our predecessors, good and bad, and the names that can still strike fear or respect into our hearts – the stories of the Canterbury Warriors.

ANNIE AND REGGIE HUDSON

Married 1919

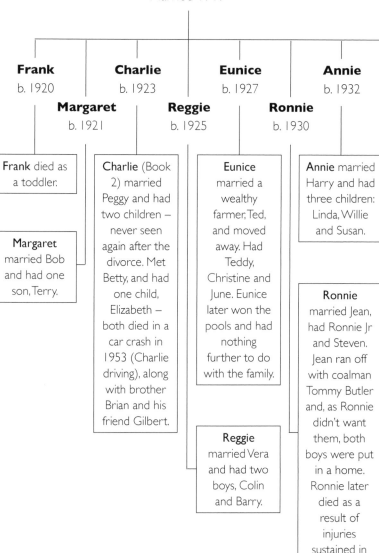

Frank
b. 1920

Charlie
b. 1923

Eunice
b. 1927

Annie
b. 1932

Margaret
b. 1921

Reggie
b. 1925

Ronnie
b. 1930

Frank died as a toddler.

Margaret married Bob and had one son, Terry.

Charlie (Book 2) married Peggy and had two children – never seen again after the divorce. Met Betty, and had one child, Elizabeth – both died in a car crash in 1953 (Charlie driving), along with brother Brian and his friend Gilbert.

Eunice married a wealthy farmer, Ted, and moved away. Had Teddy, Christine and June. Eunice later won the pools and had nothing further to do with the family.

Annie married Harry and had three children: Linda, Willie and Susan.

Ronnie married Jean, had Ronnie Jr and Steven. Jean ran off with coalman Tommy Butler and, as Ronnie didn't want them, both boys were put in a home. Ronnie later died as a result of injuries sustained in the car crash.

Reggie married Vera and had two boys, Colin and Barry.

Hudson Family Tree

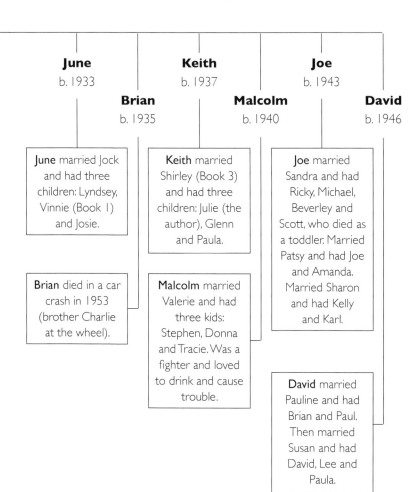

June b. 1933

Brian b. 1935

Keith b. 1937

Malcolm b. 1940

Joe b. 1943

David b. 1946

June married Jock and had three children: Lyndsey, Vinnie (Book 1) and Josie.

Brian died in a car crash in 1953 (brother Charlie at the wheel).

Keith married Shirley (Book 3) and had three children: Julie (the author), Glenn and Paula.

Malcolm married Valerie and had three kids: Stephen, Donna and Tracie. Was a fighter and loved to drink and cause trouble.

Joe married Sandra and had Ricky, Michael, Beverley and Scott, who died as a toddler. Married Patsy and had Joe and Amanda. Married Sharon and had Kelly and Karl.

David married Pauline and had Brian and Paul. Then married Susan and had David, Lee and Paula.

Prologue

November 1999

Vinnie pulled the lapels of his Crombie together and shivered. A bloody church was no place to be on a November morning. Any church, but definitely not St Joseph's Catholic Church which, built in the 1800s, made plenty of its lofty religious aims, but absolutely no concessions to comfort. And it didn't help that they'd yet to shut the doors. Every time they creaked open to admit yet another latecomer, another blast of freezing air came in too.

He glanced around him, marvelling at the size of the turnout. He was 42, so by now he'd been to a fair few funerals, but he couldn't remember the last time he'd seen the church so packed with mourners. Neither, he reflected once the service got under way, had he remembered just how long a fucking funeral mass could be. He leaned close to his mother, June, who was standing beside him, dressed in one of her trademark fur coats. 'How long is that fucking priest going to drone on for?' he whispered. 'I'm fucking freezing my bollocks off here!'

June kicked at Vinnie's boot with the toe of her black stiletto. She was 65 now, still slim, and though she was slightly less spiky than she had been in her younger days, she was still pretty feisty when she was in the mood to be. 'Vinnie! Have some respect!' she hissed, picking up her hymn book in readiness for another hymn to start. 'Bloody swearing in a church. Pack it in!'

Vinnie duly picked up his own hymn book and looked across at the coffin up in front. He'd had a good innings, had his Uncle Charlie – that was what everyone kept saying, anyway. No, 76 wasn't *that* old, but it wasn't that young either. And, truth be known, Vinnie thought, casting his eye again over the enormous congregation, he'd done fucking well to make it that far, considering. June's oldest brother, and for many years the linchpin of the whole Hudson clan, he'd flirted with death often enough to be considered lucky to have reached his seventies. And there was little doubt, though he'd be gone, that he'd not be forgotten.

The organ started up again, and Vinnie made a big show of wincing as his mam started belting out the final hymn. She could sing, no doubt about it, but he couldn't resist it. Winding her up was still a reliable source of entertainment, specially given *what* she was singing. *Make me a channel of your peace?* he thought. *As if! Are you listening to this, our Charlie?*

Vinnie glanced at the box again, unable to suppress a grin. He'd probably be turning in his coffin before he was even in the bloody grave!

He checked his watch surreptitiously as the hymn drew to a close, not wanting to risk another prodding from his mother. Not long now, hopefully, and then he could get outside and have a roll-up. And get a proper look at some of the faces he'd yet to properly clock. And there were a lot of them crammed in behind him, he knew that – all suited and booted to come here and pay their respects to his uncle, even though, ironically, many of their battle scars had probably been inflicted by the old rogue himself.

The rows in front, on the other hand, were full of close family, though you wouldn't know it – none were actually weeping. Aunties and uncles, various in-laws, and fuck knew how many cousins. Probably even a few second cousins, too – Charlie's influence had reached out far and wide. There was also the woman Vinnie knew was Charlie's latest 'companion'. She was called Dorothy Mary, and looked around the same age as his mother. Though, caked in make-up and with thick, dark arches drawn on where her eyebrows should have been, Vinnie thought she resembled some kind of old shop mannequin. He didn't know her well, but knew enough to know she was probably in a minority of one – the only one who was actually genuinely grieving for Charlie, because though his loss was sad there wasn't much grief going on, not in the traditional sense. Which was understandable, because his uncle had been something of a stranger when he died, having isolated himself from friends and family years ago.

No, this sadness today wasn't like being upset over the loss of a close relative – it was more a kind of emptiness for a time that had passed. Charlie's death represented a lost age, the end of something. Vinnie felt it and he was sure that all the others did too.

But he wasn't one for melancholy, any more than he was one for funerals. And, looking around him, he grinned to himself again. It probably wouldn't be a bad day out, this, all told. Yes, he'd had to sit through three hymns and a long boring sermon – not to mention having to listen to the divvy priest utter a load of crap about what a 'stand-up' guy Charlie was – but, looking at this lot, he realised the wake might actually be okay.

His mam had already told him it was going to be held at the Spicer Street Club, a brisk 15-minute walk away, and a place that had already played host to many family funerals, weddings and christenings. He couldn't wait to get there. Who knew? It might not just be a good knees-up. There might be a punch-up or two as well.

Slightly cheered now – due respect to his uncle notwithstanding – Vinnie picked up the order of service he'd not looked at up to now. It was a simple affair, a single sheet of paper, folded in half. On the front was a picture of St Joseph's and Charlie's birth and death dates, and on the back they'd printed a black and white photograph of the old bugger. It wasn't recent – not much danger of Charlie having posed for pictures in recent years, after all – but as Vinnie looked at it, it was like he was looking straight into the past. There were family resemblances, and there were family resemblances, and this family resemblance was staggering. *Fuck's sake!* he thought, smiling to himself as the priest rabbited on. *He looks just like me grannie Hudson in a suit!*

Or, rather, did. Now Charlie was gone, it was like something important had died with him. It was the end of an era, the likes of which they'd probably never see again. The era of the Canterbury Warriors.

Part One

Chapter I

Bradford, April 1919

8 April 1919 was a defining day in history for the city of Bradford. It also marked the end of an era. The First World War had brought many social changes. With millions of young men called up to serve their country at its outset (with many more to come, to replace the injured and fallen) millions of women had stepped in to fill the employment gap.

It had been women who'd kept the city on its feet during the crisis – taking on jobs that were definitely not considered 'women's work'. It had been women who'd toiled in factories for the war effort, too, spending long hours on assembly lines, doing laborious, dangerous work. So-called 'Canary Girls', their reward for their toil in building countless shells and missiles was the tell-tale yellow skin of jaundice, due to constantly handling explosives.

But the war had now come to an end. This was to change everything, as the young demobbed troops needed their jobs back, and little by little the women who'd kept the home fires burning were being let go and sent home to care for their men. This naturally included the transport infrastructure, and 8 April saw a major social change. It was the last day a woman would punch the tickets on Bradford's corporation trams – they wouldn't be seen again as conductors for many years.

*   *   *

8 April was also a defining day for Annie McArdle. Eighteen years old, she had weathered (and often enjoyed) the war years, but today she was about to embark on a new journey. Today was the day that she'd walk up the aisle of St Joseph's Catholic Church and vow to love, honour and obey her handsome beau, Reginald Harold Hudson, and their personal battle was about to begin.

'Aww, Annie, love,' Doris McGuire yelled as she threw a handful of rice at her old school pal. 'You know what? You look like the cat that got the cream!'

'Silly bugger!' Annie replied, ducking to try and avoid the next shower of grains winging its way towards her. She hitched up her wedding gown to save it getting blackened in the dirt. She loved her dress – it had taken her mother weeks to sew up and she felt like a queen gliding around in it. She gave Reggie's arm a quick loving squeeze. 'Here, Doris,' she joked. 'It's this fellow here that should be the one grinning. Luckiest day of his life, this is.'

'Don't show me up, woman!' Reggie snapped as they made their way down the church. 'And hell fire! I wish they'd knock it off with that bloody stuff!'

Narky bugger, Annie thought. And on their wedding day as well. Not that she was overly bothered. She knew that where Reginald was concerned she could give as good as she got – always had, always would – so he was just going to have to get used to it. They were married now and Annie intended to be just as brazen a wife as her mother had always been; not taking any nonsense off him ever.

She glanced at Reggie now, and her hand went immediately to her stomach. It was flat now – she was a slim girl – but it wouldn't be for much longer. Which was okay – their hasty marriage wouldn't seem unusual, not with all the servicemen coming home and rushing to wed the girls they'd been reunited with. But it had also shown her the kind of man Reggie was in that department; a man, to use her mother's parlance, who expected to be serviced on demand. She'd have to nip that idea in the bud quick smart.

It was amusing, though, watching Doris and the rest of her friends giving her cheeky winks – implying that she was in for a great surprise tonight. Annie snorted at the thought. She'd already had that; the surprise being that, contrary to what everyone had told her – about it being a chore and a bind that she'd just have to get used to – she'd actually enjoyed it, rather a lot.

No, she thought, the surprise would come in seven months, near as good as. But hopefully it would be a late arrival so it wasn't too blindingly obvious that she'd been such a wicked, wicked woman.

The wedding breakfast, which actually took place in the afternoon, was held at the McArdles' house. Like the Hudsons, they lived on the Broomfields estate, and in the same row of small terraced houses that they rented from the corporation.

Usually a bit of a hovel, it had put on its best face for the day – swept out and cleaned sufficiently to be smart enough to receive guests, of which there were now 30 or so, all piling in through the narrow doorway, and falling hungrily on the feast of bread and dripping Annie's mum had prepared, washed down with cupfuls of her dad's mead.

Billy McArdle's mead was a legendary tipple locally. Mostly because it was potent enough to be the cause of many a sore head, even after downing just a couple of cupfuls. Well, in today's case, as was the case when there was any sort of occasion, jarfuls – many would be drinking from washed and scrubbed jam jars, there being far too few cups to go round.

But Billy's mead was also famous because he was a bit of an enthusiast, often experimenting with flavours, depending on what kind of fruit he could nick from various gardens. Sometimes it was raspberry flavoured, other times scented with blackberry, but at this time of year there was little to add, so the wedding drink was just made with the usual honey.

'A toast! A toast!' he cried now, as he swung his mead upwards, and Annie felt her heart swell with love. She never really understood why her mam was so mean to him. To her he was a very fine man. 'To our little Queen Annie and her prince charming, Reggie Hudson,' he continued, beaming at them. 'Long may they reign!'

Annie's mum, Queenie, picked up her husband's pipe from the stone fire top and puffed on it. 'And good luck, my girl,' she called across to her daughter. She roared with laughter then. 'Because you're gonna need it. Mark my words!'

'Oh, Mam, give up,' Annie chided. 'You know he's not a wrong 'un. Well, not half as bad as some of them, anyway. And at least we'll have a roof to call our own over our heads.'

This had been a great source of pride to Annie. But an even greater source of relief. Two of her friends, Doris and Florrie, had already been married for a couple of years now, and were still living with their in-laws, all crammed in together. Hardly the most romantic way to start married life. And though she got along with Reggie's family, she certainly didn't want to live with them. She was 18 now, and sick of being treated like someone's child. No, she wanted to be in charge now – rule her *own* roost.

Queenie tutted and pointed over to Reggie. He was standing by the window, laughing and roaring with the other men. 'Really?' she said. 'Look at him! Drunk as a lord already, he is, pound to a penny. And it's not yet six o'clock.' She then smiled, giving Annie a nudge on her arm. 'Mind you, girl,' she whispered, 'if he carries on like that, at least you might miss out on a bit of how's yer father.' She winked knowingly. 'Now *that* you *can* do without!'

Annie felt her cheeks redden. How could her mam say things like that? She moved away from her. She certainly didn't want to talk about *that* sort of thing and definitely not with her mother. Not with someone who didn't have a good word to say about the man she'd supposedly once loved. No, she'd find more agreeable company with her friends. She caught her new husband's eye as she went over to join them, pleased to feel the same flutter of excitement she'd always done as their eyes met, remembering what he'd said earlier about how he loved the way she looked with her hair up, how she looked like a painting of a goddess. Slightly less agreeable was the lewd, suggestive wink he responded with, specially when he followed it up by grinning at Doris and Florrie, causing them to dissolve into a fit of giggles and blushes too.

They knew him too well, she thought, as she joined them. But then, that was probably to be expected. All four of them worked at the local Punch Bowl pub and had done for over a year now – Reggie as a waiter and with Annie, Doris and Flo serving the drinks.

'Right ladies' man, that one is,' Doris warned, as Annie took a sip from her drink. 'You'll probably have to keep him on a leash.'

The mead tasted warm in her throat. Pleasant. She took another gulp, almost downing it. 'Oh, don't you worry,' she said. 'The bugger'll be *wearing* a leash, more like.'

Flo clearly didn't want to linger on such a depressing line of thought. She stroked the arm of Annie's wedding dress and sighed. 'Aw, your gown is lovely, Annie,' she cooed. 'You look the bee's knees, you really do. Like a princess. I wish I'd had a dress like that when I married my William. We had bugger all, us, compared to this. Still don't!' She sighed then, and looked across to where her own husband was. 'And you know how folk say things like "It seems like it was only yesterday when you married him"?'

Annie nodded.

Flo stopped stroking the soft material and looked wistfully at her friend. 'Well, it doesn't. Not to me. It seems like a million years ago that *I* felt like a princess.'

'Even more reason for me to make the most of it, then!' Annie said quickly, not wanting to spoil the happy mood that was overtaking her now the mead had started taking effect. 'Look,' she said, doing a twirl so her friends could see how prettily the dress moved. 'See the way it flips up at the bottom?'

She really wasn't looking forward to having to take it off, not really. Well, she was, because Reggie would be helping her. But it still seemed a shame – seemed all wrong that once it was off, it was all over. That you only got to wear something so beautiful for a single day.

'It's just *gorgeous*,' Flo said, planting a kiss on Annie's cheek. 'And I'm so happy for you. And I bet you can't wait to get carried over that threshold later, too, Annie. Imagine that, eh? Annie McArdle with her own corporation house!'

'Annie *Hudson* now, Florrie, remember? I'm not a McArdle any more. Thank God,' she added with feeling, glancing across at her parents, and seeing them already engaged in one of their regular angry rows, probably about nothing in particular. It wasn't going to be that way with her and her Reggie. She wouldn't let it. She'd have him dancing to her tune before he even realised.

She looked at him again, not quite believing her luck. He was a catch, was her Reggie. There was no doubt about it. With his coal-black hair sleeked back so he looked like one of those film stars, his dad's posh suit fitted him perfectly. He wasn't a tall man, but he was built well, with muscles in all the right places, and looks that could melt a girl's heart.

Oh yes, Annie thought, she would have to keep an eye on this one. Right now, though, she would cut him some slack. It was supposed to be a party after all.

And it was a party that went on till midnight. One minute the house was full and it seemed the next it was suddenly empty, and Annie realised her dad was passed out on the floor while her mam was busy shoving the last remaining guest out. 'Go on, bugger off!' she was shouting, all the niceties obviously over with. 'You've all got homes to go to, haven't you?' she barked.

All but one, it seemed. The guest who'd bagged the one decent armchair and who was slumped in it, only just awake.

Her husband. 'Are you ready then, Reggie?' she asked him, shaking his shoulder. But he merely grunted and shook her arm away. 'Reggie!' she said again more sharply. 'It's time to go now!' He at least opened his eyes at this, but what Annie saw wasn't encouraging. He looked boss-eyed and could hardly keep them open.

Now sure quite how she was going to rouse him, let alone manhandle him to their house, she called Queenie over to help. 'Mam,' she called, 'come and see if you can get him up for me, will you?'

Queenie looked at him and smiled, then she shook her head at her daughter. 'You could throw a pan of water over him,' she suggested, 'but it wouldn't do you much use. No, you go on and get yourself home, girl. He's going nowhere, is he? Any more than your ruddy father. No, leave him here to sleep it off – best thing for him, really. And for you, love,' she said more gently. 'It's not often you'll have a night off, so if I were you I think I'd make the most of it.'

'I can't do that!' Annie exclaimed, mortified. 'It's my wedding night! Come on, Mam – help me at least get him on his feet.'

But her mother just looked at her sleeping son-in-law of not quite a day, tutted at Annie and shook her head again. 'You *really* want to take that lump home with you? Really? Trust me, love, even if you do manage to stagger home with him, what then? When they get into that state, it only means one of two things – either a good hiding or a bit of the other. You'll enjoy neither tonight, so go on – enjoy this last night of peace, girl, because it'll be a long time before you can enjoy another.'

Dejected by this unexpected turn in developments, yet without the energy to argue, Annie suddenly felt overcome by weariness. So she simply hitched up the hem of her dress, grabbed her mother's shawl from the door knob and made her way out of the house and towards her new home. *Have I been expecting too much?* she wondered as she traipsed through the empty streets. Was her wedding day over now? Done? Was that *it?* Because it wasn't the end to the day she'd envisaged at all. She was a bride and she was supposed to be carried over the threshold. That was the rule. Instead, she was going to have to carry herself over it – not to mention the dress she'd been so looking forward to Reggie helping her out of – and go to bed, in the cold, all alone. He might be drunk but at least he'd have made a half-decent hot-water bottle. Not to mention the rest of it, as well.

All those dreams she'd had about what was going to happen tonight, where were they now? They were going to dance around the house together – and as they danced, he was going to sing to her. Mouth her favourite song – 'I'm Forever Blowing Bubbles' – into her ear. He was going to sing that and then he was going to sweep her off to bed, just as he'd swept her off her feet when she'd first met him. Then they'd cuddle up together under the covers, on the lovely horsehair mattress that her dad had got for them specially, and watch the light of the moon from their bedroom window.

But not now! she thought angrily as she stomped across the grass, the moon above her shining brightly as if to spite her. She was all alone, and it was all wrong, and it wouldn't be happening again. *You're a bloody shower, Reggie Hudson!* she huffed to herself as she approached the dark house. This bloody marriage was going to see some changes. That was a promise.

Chapter 2

1923

Annie stretched out her spine, pressing her palms against her hips and groaning. Trying to scrub her step, even from a squatting position, was really the last thing she should be doing in her condition. Not right now. Not with this niggle in her back all the time. And given how much of an effort it had taken even to get down on her haunches, she decided, it would be as nothing compared to the effort it would take to pull herself back up.

Her lower back was hurting now, really quite badly, and a ripple of anxiety ran through her. She was ten days past term now and something told her that the baby inside her knew it. That it was just waiting, the little bleeder, for the worst possible moment, which, given she was out the front, attempting to get down far enough to scrub her front step, might just be now.

She bent back to her task again, scouring swiftly, anxious to finish now. Anxious to have everything ready for when this little one came into the world. Would she be blessed with a boy this time? She hoped so.

Not that she didn't love her little Margaret, her precious daughter, who had probably saved her. But she really wanted a boy this time. For Reggie.

She'd been punished. She knew that. They both had. Punished by a vengeful God, for their wickedness before they'd married. He'd taken their firstborn, their dear little son, Frank, conceived out of wedlock and born just eight and a half months after. Snatched him from them before he was even a year old.

She could hardly bear to bring the pictures of that day to mind, even now. If she so much as *thought* about it – and she couldn't help but think about it, what with a new baby imminent – the images would tumble in, swirling round and round her head, making her feel so sick and panicky that it was all she could do to try and shoo them away again. And it wasn't like it had been a disease that had taken him, either. It had been an apple, just a ruddy piece of apple, that was all, that had done for her cherished firstborn. Choked him dead – killing him even as she watched. There'd been nothing anyone could have done – they'd all said that to her, everyone. Reggie too, but Annie still felt he blamed her.

Didn't matter anyway. She'd been punished, and that was all there was to it. Reggie could never blame her as much as she blamed herself.

Annie gave up, puffing as she rose again, and glared at her next-door neighbour. It was always the same: Agnes Flanagan, queen of the perfect ox-blood doorstep, happily scrubbing away at hers with a stiff wire brush, getting a right lather on it with her trusty bar of soap. 'You'll scrub the bloody paint off if you carry on,' Annie said, feeling an irrational amount of irritation that, right now, at least, she couldn't have a nice, sparkling step too.

But she couldn't – not with a belly the size of a baby hippo. With a belly, in fact, full of *this bloody baby* – where was it? Hopefully on its way, she thought, feeling her back twinge again.

'Oh, be quiet, Annie,' Agnes snapped. 'Stop being such an old sourpuss. It's jealousy is what it is, plain and simple. You're only narked because you know your old man will notice mine's the cleanest.'

Reggie wouldn't. Annie knew that. He probably couldn't have cared less. Wouldn't even notice, because these days he seemed to prefer his time at the bloody pub. So much for the honeymoon ruddy period. Even so, just Agnes thinking that he might made Annie annoyed with her. If she hadn't been so immobile she might have leapt the fence separating them and given Agnes a slap – just for being as annoying as she always was.

Which she had been, ever since they'd moved in two years back. An Irish couple in their thirties, they couldn't have kids, apparently. Which meant they didn't have any kids cluttering up their house, which for some reason seemed to make them feel superior. And it meant she had time, did Agnes Flanagan, something Annie sorely lacked. Time to have the cleanest windows, the shiniest step, the tidiest garden.

But she'd show the Flanagans. Show everyone, in fact. Once this little one was born, she'd *definitely* show them. They'd been talking about it, and Reggie had made her a promise – to dig up the garden and lay some turf for a proper lawn. Annie couldn't wait to see the old cow's face when she saw that.

'Shut your cakehole, Agnes,' she said now, anxious to get her own jibe in. 'If your old man had a job, maybe he wouldn't have the time to spend on women's work. You only come out to the step so you can do your gossiping. It doesn't even *need* cleaning. Stan only painted it again last week.'

'Oh, my old man should get a job, should he?' Agnes huffed, standing up now the better to waggle a finger in Annie's direction. She was fond of doing that. Assuming the ten or so years that separated them gave her permission to carry on like she was Annie's mother. 'I'll have you know, girl,' she added, 'that he has a chance of a *great* job. The railways are setting on and he's been told he's in with a chance. Now, that's a *job*,' she said, pausing to let the emphasis sink in. 'Hmm, let me see … What is it your man does now? Oh yes, that's right. He waits on up at the Punch Bowl, doesn't he? When he's not up there blind drunk, that is.'

Annie flinched as the pain left her back and gripped her abdomen. Gripped it hard, like a fist. Like a vice. Oh, how she wanted to fly for the old witch next door, but now definitely wasn't the time. She was in labour. She knew the signs. And she knew time was short – little Margaret had been so quick she'd fairly fallen out. So instead, she leaned towards her neighbour and gripped the fencing between the houses. 'Agnes! Go get the midwife, will you?'

Her neighbour's demeanour changed instantly. 'Oh, Annie,' she said, looking anxious now. 'Is it your time? Is it the baby?' She dropped the brush and raised her hands to her cheeks. 'Oh, sweet Jesus, what'll I do?'

'Just get the bloody midwife!' Annie screamed as it hit her very forcefully that the pains were coming quicker now, and that her little one was spark out in her cot indoors, oblivious. 'Then come straight back here and watch our Margaret for me!' she added, trying to keep her legs from buckling. 'Don't stand there looking gormless, Agnes. Go!'

Agnes seemed to get the message then, abandoning the soap as well as the brush, then running down her path and out onto the estate. Thankfully, the local midwife only lived a few streets away and if there were no other babies being born that day – and fingers crossed there wouldn't be – Agnes would find her home and ready to be called out.

Feeling reasonably calm now she knew help was on the way, Annie supported herself using the wall, and waited for the latest pain to subside before staggering back into the house. Once there she knew she had to try and think straight. Margaret was still asleep, curled into a comma in the cot Reggie had made for her, and for a moment or two Annie dithered about waking her. It was almost dinner-time though, and she'd soon be needing a feed. And if things started moving quickly, there'd be no chance of giving her one.

Decided, Annie moved towards the cot. She had to nurse her. And quickly, before the next contraction came – she knew only too well that it might be hours before she was fit enough to do it later. Groaning with the effort, she hauled her daughter from the cot, bringing the blankets with her, then settled into the big chair, better to get her breast out from under her pinny. 'Come on, baby,' she soothed to the semi-conscious toddler. 'Shh, there, come on. Time you had your tea.'

Margaret was angry. And so she would be. She'd been disturbed from her slumbers. She kicked and fussed, at first refusing to take the breast. 'Come on, you little bugger,' Annie soothed, wincing as Margaret's teeth clamped round her tender skin. 'Make the most of it. You'll be having to share it soon. Either that, or it'll be down to the wet nurse with you,' she gently joked. 'And knowing her, it'll come out sour!'

Margaret relaxed eventually and started to suckle, but as the pain started building again Annie knew it wouldn't last – and, sure enough, as Annie writhed beneath her, Margaret snapped her head back angrily. 'Mammy, no!' she yelled, smacking Annie's breast hard and kicking her. 'Want bread! Want *bread*!'

'Hush, Margaret,' Annie soothed, trying to keep her voice from rising. The pain deep within her was becoming unbearable. If she didn't coax her daughter down now, she'd end up falling off anyway. It was just so hard to sit, when she felt compelled to bear down. It was coming. There was no doubt. It was coming.

'Down you get,' she said, gently urging Margaret to climb off of her. 'Baby's coming now. Remember Mammy's baby in her tummy? Baby's coming now –'

'Baby?' Margaret's glass-blue eyes widened. 'Baby, baby, baby!'

She shuffled down now, energised, and ran towards the cold hearth. 'Baby!' she squealed, picking up a stray piece of coal, scribbling on lino with it as Annie convulsed in pain again.

She needed to be down there with her daughter, Annie realised. There was no point in even thinking about her bed now. She needed to be down on the floor where Margaret was. And quickly.

This wasn't the way I'd planned it! she thought irritably, lifting her skirt.

Agnes and the midwife rushed into the living room together, just at the point when Charles Hudson made his entrance. He slithered out, huge and glistening – a ten pounder, it turned out – and with a pair of lungs any town crier would have been proud of.

'Oh! It's a little boy, Annie!' Agnes cried, her voice breaking. 'A little gift from God to replace your Frank.'

Agnes had never known Frank. She and Stan had moved into their house in Broomfields a while after he'd died, but Annie knew her neighbour's emotion was genuine, and felt an unexpected rush of warmth towards her. She felt like crying too, her eyes filling with tears as she held both her babies, wishing above all that Reggie were home to hold his son. She gazed down at the angry pink bundle swaddled close to her chest. He'd be the light of Reggie's life, she just knew it.

Chapter 3

1932

Charlie was a handsome boy. Everybody said so, especially the women. And he knew it, too. He'd heard it said often enough.

'Ooh, your Charlie's gonna be a heartbreaker!' he'd hear them say to his mam. 'Ooh, look at those eyes of his!' they'd coo. 'Look at that lovely head of hair!' Then they'd ruffle it and mess it up, which annoyed him.

His hair was black, like his dad's. His eyes were greeny-blue, like his mam's. He'd look at himself in the chipped bit of mirror propped above the basin in the scullery, and he'd wonder what it was about his face that was so special. Because it clearly was. The girls in school were always trying to hug and kiss him, and if he rewarded them with a smile they'd squeal in delight.

It was different with the men, and especially with his father, who didn't seem to trust him. Charlie never understood what it was that his dad disliked about him – was it because he wasn't Frank? The baby that had come before and died? He didn't know, but he felt it and it stung. Reggie either completely ignored him – sometimes it was like he didn't even exist – or he'd pay him rather more attention than made Charlie strictly comfortable, always trying to catch him out doing something wrong, so he could give him a thump or a whack with his leather belt.

'A sneaky bugger.' Charlie had heard his dad call him that once. Which had hurt him, because he didn't even know what he'd done wrong. But it had been all right, because he'd said it to his mam, and she'd given him hell for it. She always did. She was like an animal – his protector, was how he always thought of it. Oh, if she copped his dad giving him the belt for no reason she'd lay into him good and proper, would his mam.

As well as waiting on at the Punch Bowl, which he'd done ever since Charlie could remember, his dad earned a few bob from boxing. He'd do it at the Spicer Street Club, where, unbeknown to the police, they would throw open their back doors and happily host a fight – and between anyone who thought they could throw a punch. It was a nice earner for the landlord, because he'd take bets from the crowd, providing a pot to be shared between him and the winner.

Much as he disliked his father, Charlie loved being taken to watch a fight with him. Boxing was in his blood, and it enthralled him. For as long as he could remember he had watched his dad training in the back yard, punching away at a huge home-made punch bag that was hung from an enormous hook fixed into the house wall. Charlie had even watched his mam make it; it was actually a coal sack that she'd filled with pieces of old lino that had been scraped up, bit by bit, from his grandmother's kitchen floor.

Charlie trained too. He'd begun when he was three. The linoleum in the sack hurt his knuckles like mad, but he'd soon worked out that it was the one time when his dad would give him *his* time, so if he'd had his way he'd have punched away all day.

And boxing was the one thing that made his dad proud of him. Never prouder than when he heard Reggie telling his mam, 'That kid's gonna be the next Jack Dempsey'.

*   *   *

'Where've you been?' Annie said now, pulling pins from her hair. 'You should have been in half an hour back. We're in a hurry. We're off to Spicer Street. Your dad's taking on Billy Brennan today and it's worth a lot of money.'

It was a Friday afternoon and Charlie was just home from school. He was tired – no matter how long his legs got, the three-mile walk was never less than punishing come a Friday – but this was the best news he'd had all day.

'I met some mates and we had a kick around,' he said by way of explanation, lingering for a moment to watch his mam doing her hair. It was black like his and his dad's but soft where theirs was wiry, and he loved watching her doing it, seeing how she magically made it change, sliding the pins out that she'd put in the night before, in tight little crosses, to reveal curls that would spring out and fall onto her shoulders in big lazy S shapes. He thought she was beautiful and he was glad when people said they could see her in him. She was like a movie star, especially when she put petroleum jelly on her eyebrows. It made her look like that actress Greta Garbo.

'D'ya think me dad will win, Mam?' he asked her now.

She grinned. 'He better do, son,' she said, pulling her pink cardigan over her shoulders. 'I've got all my mates betting on him. Now go on, go upstairs and get changed, then come back down and wash your face. We have to go.'

Charlie ran upstairs. He'd been the last one home, he knew, but, bar his mam, the house was empty. His big sister Margaret would have taken the rest off to the park, and she'd be giving them their bread and jam after as well. He had lots of brothers and sisters now – they seemed to keep arriving all the time. As well as Margaret, there was young Reggie, who was eight now, and Eunice, who was five, then two-year old Ronnie and little Annie who was still a baby. There was another one coming too, but not till next year, his mam had told him. And he was glad it wasn't yet, because he didn't know where they'd fit. His gran always said there was no room to swing a cat in their house, and he agreed. They were all packed in just like sardines.

But this afternoon was his, and as he ran into the bedroom he felt a familiar sense of excited anticipation. When Reggie was nine he'd be allowed to come too, but for the moment, at least, going to the boxing was Charlie's treat alone.

And as he pulled off his jumper, he also had a brain wave. The week before, he had earned a small fortune – a whole thruppence – for running betting slips around the estate for Mr Cappovanni. Mr Cappovanni was a bookie and his family came from Italy, and Charlie had done work for him for a while now.

Not that he let on quite how much he'd been getting. No, he usually hid it, where it was out of harm's reach, on this occasion inside a rip in the mattress upstairs. His dad only earned a pound and 12 shillings at the Punch Bowl, so Charlie knew if he knew about it he'd be after getting his hands on it, so he could blow it on beer for him and Annie. So Charlie constantly came up with new places to hide his earnings so he could be sure they'd still be there when he went to find them.

Today, Charlie had a plan for those hard-earned three pennies. He'd use them to place a secret bet with Mr Cappovanni on Billy Brennan. He'd heard about him – heard things that hardly anyone else knew. That, for all his front, Billy Brennan was barely managing to keep his family from starving – so Charlie knew he had an awful lot to fight for. Reggie, on the other hand, was just in it for the booze. His dad was good, yes, but this fight was really no contest, not as far as Charlie was concerned.

He finished changing and turned his attention to retrieving the money. The kids' bedroom was one of only two in the house, and in this one you probably couldn't even swing a rat. Not that there was a bed in it; just an old mattress which almost filled the room, set directly on the floor and on which all of the children had to sleep. It stank – of sweat and piss, and other even more revolting things, and was covered in coats, pullovers and scraps of material.

Charlie was lucky, though. He and young Reg, being the oldest boys, at least had an outside edge apiece. Margaret would squeeze up next to Reggie – though she'd often get out and sleep on the floor instead – and all the younger ones ended up in the middle. Here they could piss away all night if they wanted to, because they only got it all over each other.

Charlie held his breath as he glanced at the sunken middle bit of the bed now. Sodden and stinking, it was also crawling with maggots; something he tried hard not to think about at night, but couldn't escape being reminded of now. He carefully retrieved his savings from the hole in the side and then ran out of the room and back downstairs to scrub his face clean at the kitchen sink.

Annie was waiting in the hallway for him once he was done, and she smiled. 'Ahh,' she said, kissing the top of his head, 'you are a bonnie lad when you're nice and clean, Charlie Hudson. You, er, wouldn't happen to have a spare bob or two for your mam, would you, son?'

Charlie smiled back at her, feigning innocence with ease. 'No, Mam,' he said. 'Sorry. Mr Cappovanni lost money this week. I might get summat next week, though, if I work hard.'

He didn't feel guilty deceiving her. Not on this occasion anyway. His mam would only have used it to bet on his dad, and as far as he was concerned old Reggie boy was going to take a tumble.

*   *   *

Knowing the pennies were in his pocket put a spring in Charlie's step as he walked with his mam down the street, past the big mill and then across the fields to the club. Cappovanni would definitely be going to the fight, he knew, and that was good because he'd be sure to keep the bet a secret. Billy Brennan was the underdog and when he took his dad down – which he would – Charlie would be in for a tidy profit. Which felt fair, too. He worked very hard for Cappovanni and he knew his employer was proud of him. Proud that he always kept his mouth shut, and also proud that he knew everything about everyone on the large estate where they lived.

The back room of the club was already full of people when he and his mam arrived, thick with smoke, and with a rumble of excitement in the air. It was 5 p.m. now and the fight was due to start soon – it had to be, so it could be all over and done with by the time the club officially opened at seven. He couldn't see his dad, but knew he was probably limbering up in the toilets – that's where the fighters went to change into their shorts. He could, however, see Mr Cappovanni. He was moving among the people, looking like any other person, but Charlie, who knew what to look out for in such matters, knew he was discreetly taking bets.

He'd followed his mam to the bar, and now tugged at her sleeve. 'Mam, is it okay if I go talk to Mr Cappovanni?' he asked Annie.

She ordered herself a gill of beer before turning to him. 'Yes, go on then,' she said, 'but, Charlie, you be careful, son. That fellow breaks legs to them that owe him. If anything starts, I want you right back with me, you hear?'

Charlie promised he would, then ran off towards his mentor. His dad might have taught him all he knew about boxing, but Mr Cappovanni knew about all sorts of other, more interesting things, like running books, protection rackets, extortion. And as far as Charlie was concerned these were the things you really needed to know about, and Mr Cappovanni was the man from whom he'd learn them.

'Can you put this on Billy for me, Mr Cappovanni?' Charlie whispered as he got near enough. 'Only don't tell me mam or dad, will you?'

He slipped the pennies into the bookie's dark, wrinkled hand and watched as his fingers closed over them.

Cappovanni was in his mid-fifties, and though nobody knew for sure, it was generally assumed he had a connection with the Mafia. This alone seemed to be enough to strike fear into the hearts of his enemies, and whether it was true or not, there was no doubt he was a force to be reckoned with; where the Depression kept the rest of the country in poverty and rags, Albert Cappovanni had risen to the top – like a great beast rising from a sea of grime.

He stared hard at Charlie for a moment, skewering him under his gaze. Then laughed out loud. 'My, my, kiddo,' he said, 'I'll make a man out of you yet! And don't worry,' he added under his breath, 'I'll keep it quiet, son, but one thing.' His eyes narrowed and he leaned down towards Charlie. 'Don't you go telling anyone else you've gone against your old man, will you? Or I'll have to alter my odds. My old lady'll have me guts for garters if I don't go home on top.'

Which was something Charlie couldn't imagine Mr Cappovanni's wife *ever* doing, but he promised he wouldn't and scampered happily back to his mam.

The fight was due to start very soon after. The club was heaving now, the air tinged with blue from all the pipe smoke and from those lighting up Players Navy cigarettes. The men had formed a ring now around Reggie and Billy, while the few women that were there hung back and chatted by the bar. This obviously included his mam, so Charlie was free to enjoy the fight, even more so when Mr Cappovanni scooped him up and gave him the perfect vantage point sitting on his shoulders. From here he'd cheer for his dad, obviously, shouting along with all his mates, but all the while hoping his long shot would pay off. Which to his mind wasn't even that much of a long shot. His dad might be the favourite, but Charlie was sharp. He had eyes and ears and the reason he knew about Billy Brennan was because he never wasted an opportunity to use them.

It was exciting but at the same time sometimes difficult to watch. It was his dad, after all, and this was a bare-knuckle fight. They always were. Gloves and padding were generally considered to be for sissies, so blood, snot and spit splatters were the norm, and he winced as he watched the blows raining down, as the two men pummelled the life out of each other.

He took careful note though and, as each round ended – with the ringing of a bell – he made a mental note of the way things were going. And it soon became clear that his dad wasn't going to win. Billy Brennan, as Charlie'd anticipated, was like a raging animal in the impromptu ring, screaming and running at Reggie as if protecting his young, which, in a way, was what he was there to do. And though Reggie tried to mirror every punch, and often succeeded, he was never going to be a match for a desperate starving man. The fight was all over in 20 minutes.

As Charlie's dad threw the towel in Charlie himself glanced around, and it was clear most of the bets had been on Reggie. Most of the onlookers looked as defeated as the fighter they'd backed, throwing down their chitties and grumbling to each other. Not that anyone would say a word to Charlie's dad. They wouldn't dare. His adrenalin still pumping, Reggie always had a punch in reserve for after a fight, and it would still be in his blood when they got home as well. A good time to do a disappearing act, Charlie thought.

After watching his parents sink a few more morose gills, Charlie was glad when it was time to go home. He'd done well – he'd won a shilling – turned his three pennies into 12, all thanks to his bet with Mr Cappovanni, though it was money he'd not have to worry about hiding; he'd have it off him at a more sensible time. But there would be a price to pay for his dad's loss, even though it wasn't him that was responsible, and as they walked up the path he could tell even without looking that his mam would be watching his dad, trying to gauge his mood.

He glanced up to see Margaret peering hopefully out of the window, knowing she'd work it out for herself even before he shook his head. It was the same every time his dad had a fight, always had been. If he won, they'd be linking arms, giggling and stupid – blind drunk, the pair of them, but in a good way. Those times the kids would all get a treat, too. If he lost, though, they would still be blind drunk, but scowling at each other and usually arguing all the way home. The kids knew there'd be no treat on those occasions.

This was one of those occasions. 'Why are you all still up?' Reggie roared as he staggered into the front room. He lunged at Margaret and tried to grab her but she ducked. 'Come here, you little get!' he yelled. 'I hope you've made us some tea, girl – and get these bleeding nippers up to bed!'

Margaret kept her composure. She always did. Charlie imagined she always would. 'There's some dripping in the back room, dad,' she said, 'and some tea on the range. Shall I get you some?' she ventured, trying to pacify him.

Annie, being drunk, was less civilised. 'Oh, so you're a big man *now*, are you, Reggie Hudson? Not so bloody big in the club, were you? Don't you dare take it out on these children!'

Reggie spun round and landed a slap on the side of Annie's head. 'Keep it shut, Annie, I'm warning you,' he growled. 'You're a wicked woman. Always was, always will be.'

Annie drew herself up, just as she always did, and Charlie knew what was coming. 'I promise you on my life, Reggie, I'll leave you, I will! I'll pack my things and take the kids and go back to my mother's. I'm not standing for this every bloody week.'

Charlie's heart sank. He knew what was coming next as well. As did the others. You could see it on their faces. Little Eunice quickly scooped up baby Annie and backed away towards the fireplace. 'It's all right, Dada,' she said. 'We'll be good an' we'll all go to bed now. Look, Dada – our little Annie is smiling at you.'

'No!' Reggie yelled, glaring at Annie. 'It's bloody not all right! Come on, the lot of you, line up. Your mother is leaving, is she? Well, let's just see, eh? Come on – you too, Charlie. You get over here right *now*. Right. One at a time, then. Come on,' he roared. 'Who are you going to live with?'

It was the same almost every weekend. Were they going to pick him or were they going to pick her? Too much beer and not enough to eat – that was what Agnes next door always used to say. All this nonsense for a bit of bread. And she should know, Charlie thought miserably, as he took his place in line. She heard every word, every time.

The outcome never differed, either. The young ones would cry and refuse to answer, which would only make their father worse; he'd take his belt off and would wave it around, sometimes clipping one or two of them, threatening them with it till they'd all made their choice. And between them, the kids tried their best to make it fair. One by one, they'd alternate, half choosing Annie, the other Reggie, but whatever they did, and whoever they chose, it still earned all of them a crack. Still saw them sent off to bed without any supper. And in Charlie's case, without any tea either.

'Stop that snivelling,' Charlie ordered as his brothers and sisters clambered across the freezing cold mattress. 'It'll do you no good and it won't get you any supper either. Listen,' he added, lowering his voice, just in case the rowing downstairs stopped, 'I've earned some wages tonight, so if you shut up and be good, I'll get you all some sugar and cocoa tomorrow.'

The grins on his siblings' faces felt like riches to Charlie. Even Margaret smiled – something she didn't do often, especially when her mam and dad started up the way they had. Charlie felt happier now. Tomorrow, like he'd promised, he'd treat them – make them all cones out of some folded-up bits of newspaper, share the spoils and watch them lick their fingers in and dip to their hearts' content.

Then tonight, just like always, would be forgotten.

Chapter 4

1940

Annie lit a cigarette and drew deeply on it as she sat down on the doorstep for a moment's rest. It had been an exhausting morning and would be an equally exhausting afternoon, and as she watched Reggie and the boys disappear round the corner with the last of the family's belongings, all she could think of was the mess that she'd be faced with when she got to the other end.

They were moving today, after 22 years. To the brand new estate that was currently being built in Little Horton, to provide homes for the growing population. And they'd been lucky, in a way – the Broomfields estate was going to be being demolished over the next couple of years and, as a growing family, they'd got priority for getting the first of the built homes.

'You all set then, fanny Annie?' Agnes Flanagan asked as she stepped out of her own door. 'Sure, you and your tribe won't want to know us now you've got yourself a three bedroomed.'

Annie blew out smoke in a thin stream and shook her head. She must be getting old. She couldn't recall a time when she'd last felt so bone-weary. 'I've nothing to brag about, Agnes,' she said, pointing down to her pregnant belly. 'Nine children now, one in the graveyard and this one on its way. A three bedroomed might give us a bit more room, but once this one shows up I doubt we'll even notice.'

Annie smiled at her neighbour of over two decades. They'd
rubbed along okay, all told, she and Agnes. Many didn't. And
as for the house itself, they went back even longer. She remembered back to that first night – her first as Mrs Hudson, and
how she'd turned up at it without Mr Hudson even in tow. Him
passed out at her mother's, her alone in the cold bed, all teary
– so frightened about what the future might hold.

The future had certainly brought plenty of children. Child
after child, each leaving Annie more weathered and weary
than the last. Hundreds of scraped knees to be kissed, and as
many set-tos with the neighbours' kids … And their parents,
too, when fights had broken out …

She felt tearful again all of a sudden. 'I'm going to miss this
place, Agnes. I don't know …' She shook her head. 'It might
be grand and that up there, but I'm worried I won't settle. I
belong *here*. It's all I'm used to.'

Agnes climbed over the sagging fence and joined Annie on
the step. 'Ah, go on with you, Annie. It's no use getting all
maudlin, is it? I hear Canterbury estate is fit for the toffs, and
the houses have all you could wish for. Does yours have a fixed-
in bath? Doris Coulson said hers had a bath. Fixed to the floor,
she said, with running water. Think of it! Mind you,' she said,
after a moment's pondering, 'Doris Coulson also said her old
man had joined the war, didn't she? Bloody liar she is. Everyone
knows he ran off with a scarlet woman!'

Annie laughed. For all their spats, Agnes could always cheer
her up. All those years. All that history. She was going to miss
her. 'Yes, Agnes,' she said, 'we'll be having a fixed-in bath. We
have our own toilet too.' This was a detail that did make her
happy. She'd spent 22 years using a toilet in the block down the
back – each block serving four of the terraced houses. To not
have to trudge to it would feel like such a luxury. 'It's right

there in our own back yard,' she said. 'Imagine.' She put her cigarette out and stroked her hands over her swollen belly. 'Particularly when you're in my condition, eh?' She turned to grin at Agnes. 'I sometimes wish my Reggie would find himself a scarlet woman. Give someone else a belly full of arms and legs for a change.'

The two women laughed and spent a companionable ten minutes reminiscing. That was a safer place, Annie thought, the past. She was eight months gone and before she knew it there would be another mouth to feed. Another nipper to care for in an increasingly uncertain world.

Times were changing and Annie really didn't like it. A lot of the local men had already been called up to fight in the war and she was afraid Charlie might be called next. He was almost 18 now, after all, so there'd be nothing to be done about it – and no chance of talking him out of it if he *was* called – but he was still her baby and she was frightened she might lose him.

There was danger at home too; Bradford had already seen more than one air raid; this new kind of war was being brought right to their doorsteps. Rawson Market had taken a hit, and though it hadn't been that serious, it was enough to put the frighteners on people. And it looked like the powers that be were expecting worse. Thousands of kiddies in other cities were in the process of being evacuated to safer areas. Would that be happening in Bradford too? They kept saying not – kept saying the bombs in Bradford were just off-target, but Annie didn't think she could bear it if they took her kids away.

But better be safe than sorry anyway. The best thing about moving to the new estate, as far as Annie was concerned, was that because they had one of the bigger houses on the end of a street they had an Anderson shelter in their garden.

'You'll have to come down to ours, Agnes,' Annie said, 'if you hear the sirens. Just come straight down to us. You'll be safe in our bomb shelter.'

Agnes wiped her face with a corner of her pinny. Annie squeezed her arm. Were those tears in the old girl's eyes? 'Bless you, Annie,' Agnes said, 'that's kind. But the ruddy Germans won't have me running. If the good Lord sees fit to blow me to smithereens, then that's what'll happen.'

Annie believed her, too. She was going to miss her old friend.

Annie had just hauled herself back up onto her feet when a sound from down the road heralded the arrival of a cart.

She waved. Reggie, Charlie and young Reggie were back from having taken round the last cartload of possessions, dragging the now empty cart behind them. They all looked hot and sweaty in the late August sun. Agnes stood up too. 'Will I get you some water, lads?' she called. 'I'll go tell Stan that you're back with the cart.'

The cart had been a gift for the house move. Without it, the two-mile trips back and forth would have been interminable. Stan had made it himself, toiling away for long hours the previous year. It had been part of a plan he'd formed with a friend called Tinker Mick, who lived in a gypsy wagon on some spare land by Peel Park. Being a Romany, he also had a horse – a big black mare called Ebony, who'd seen better days. But she was still a strong working horse, even so. So the two of them had decided to pool their resources and see if they could get into the coal business.

But that was before the war. Everything, coal included, was in very short supply now, so though the horse still had her uses the cart had been made redundant. Handy, though, Annie thought, for the business of moving house, as long as you had men strong enough to drag it about.

The cart parked up, Reggie leaned against the wall to get his breath back. He was still as fit as a butcher's dog, and still had the same twinkle in his eye, but it had been a hard job hauling so much stuff all that way, and Annie could see he was knackered.

'Been better if the lazy bum had seen fit to give us a hand,' he grumbled, as he and Annie stepped back inside for a last look around. She couldn't quite believe the whole street was being demolished, but that was all it was probably fit for, even so.

'You about ready to make a move, woman of mine?' Reggie asked Annie.

'I am that,' Annie said, taking a last lingering look. Seeing it empty now seemed to bring about a change in her. No sense in looking back, she thought, the empty room already closing in on her – she had to look forwards. And the thought of that fixed-in bath dragged her out of her melancholy. 'Yes,' she said, meaning it. 'Yes, I'm good and ready. Can't wait to get out of this place, truth be told.'

Back out front, Agnes had returned with jam jars full of water for the lads, and Annie looked on proudly as Charlie took one from her and downed it in one. He was a fine lad, was her Charlie. He'd be a fine man as well.

'Thanks, auntie Aggie,' he said, winking. 'I'll miss you when we're gone.'

Agnes blushed. She was soft on him. Always had been. Always would be. The son she'd never had, perhaps? Though she'd never let on. 'Ah, go on, lad,' she said, 'an' you be sure to watch over them young 'uns for your ma, hear me?' She gestured towards Annie's belly. 'Specially when she's pushing that latest one out.'

Young Reggie winced, which made Annie smile. He was at
that age when anything to do with women having babies made
him do that. Not so slow when it came to girls, though, she
thought, smiling to herself.

'Come on, then,' his father ordered – now *he'd* been that age
for ever. 'Let's be off, then. We've still a day's work to do down
at the other place.'

In half a day, Annie thought, gathering her bag and a stray
baby's rattle she'd retrieved from the hedge earlier. Then she
took Charlie's arm and they set off in the warm August
sunshine, the thought of that bath, and having a soak in it,
making the walk just that little easier.

But today? *Yes*, she thought to herself, already knowing the
answer. *And some say pigs fly, Annie Hudson.*

Charlie was glad to get to the new place and to know his day
was over. He'd been hard at it since early morning, and as far
as he was concerned had done his bit. He had somewhere to be
now – a meet with old Mr Cappovanni. To discuss a boxing
match he was taking part in the following month.

Mr Cappovanni was more of his manager now, whenever
the opportunity arose – something that tickled Charlie no end.
It made him feel like more of a professional, and had changed
the dynamic between them. He even fought under the new
name of Tucker Hudson. He had no idea why, but that was the
name his grandfather had been known by and, according to Mr
Cappovanni, it was a proper boxer's name.

And Charlie, more than anything, wanted to be a proper
boxer. And he'd made a good start as well; though he'd not yet
had many serious fights, he'd won every one that he'd had.

Which was good, but, from the financial point of view, it
wasn't *that* good, because it didn't really leave much of an

opportunity for the bookies taking bets on an outcome. Charlie wondered what Mr Cappovanni might have in mind for his next fight. For him to throw it? It was possible. He'd already talked about it. The question was, was it something Charlie should agree to? He'd have to see. Money was always in such chronically short supply. He decided he might consider it – for a price.

Right now, though, standing in the doorway of one of the three upstairs bedrooms, Charlie's thoughts were on more workaday things – such as the mess in the bedroom before him. It felt strange having a new house – everything gleaming and perfect – and then filling it with all their grimy, battered possessions. But it could have been worse. They at least had a bit of space now. And having three bedrooms made one extremely important difference. It meant that, at long last, the children could be separated into the sexes. Charlie, Reggie, Ronnie, Brian and little Keith would go into the bigger room – the one he was standing in, and Margaret, Eunice, Annie and June would share the one opposite. And the boys had done better in the bed stakes as well. While the girls had to use the filthy smelly mattress they'd brought with them, Annie had managed to beg a new one from the church for the boys. Well, not exactly new – it had apparently belonged to another parishioner, who'd died. But not while actually on it, Annie had quickly reassured them.

It was still a squash, though, and if Charlie had one wish about his mam's pregnancy it was that whatever came out at the end of it was a girl. It was hard enough trying to sleep sharing a mattress as it was; throw in a new baby and he might as well say goodbye to sleep at all. Not the best training for a professional boxer.

* * *

It was just two weeks after the move when he had an answer to that question. It was early September now and most of the kids were back in school. Charlie and Reggie, however, too old for school these days, had been told that on no account were they to do a disappearing act, as their dad was at work and their mam was getting close now. Enjoying the peace and quiet that had been enforced on them – they were jointly in charge of minding their baby brother – they were boxing in the back garden, cheered on by little Keith, who was just three.

They heard Margaret coming out before they saw her.

'Quick, Charlie!' she said briskly, beckoning them to come back inside. 'It's time. One of you needs to go for the midwife.'

Margaret was normally at work too – she was a machinist down at Brigella Mills – but she'd decided not to go in so she could keep an eye on their mam. She'd already looked like she might be starting that morning.

'Go on, you go, Reggie,' Charlie said. 'I'll stay here and mind our Keith. And if she's not in, you know the drill, don't you?'

Reggie nodded. He knew the drill because they all did. Emma the midwife, who lived round in Nene Street, was a familiar face around the whole of their part of Bradford, and over the years had brought most of the local kids into the world. And if she wasn't home, she had a piece of slate propped on her doorstep, on which she'd chalk the addresses of all the women she'd planned on visiting that day. That way, if she was needed, there was always a way to find her, though, more often than not, she was usually found out and about, going from patient to patient on her shiny black tricycle.

Having delivered her orders, Margaret went back inside to look after Annie, so there was nothing for Charlie and Keith to do but wait. There was certainly no point in running down to the Punch Bowl to fetch his dad back from work; Big Reggie, as people had taken to calling him since little Reggie'd been born, had no truck with men getting involved in such things. He'd come home, there'd be another nipper, and that would be that, something Charlie didn't really understand. Why did he keep on giving his mama all these babies if he couldn't be bothered with them when they came?

'You want to fight me?' he asked Keith now. 'Punch me lights out, little man?'

Being the baby, little Keith got lots of attention from his brothers and sisters, but by this time tomorrow, Charlie thought, that would change. Though not from him – he had a real soft spot for his little firecracker of a brother. He was scrawny as a chicken but he had a confident way about him – a certain chippiness that always made Charlie smile. Perhaps he'd make a fighter of him yet.

He lifted his fists. 'Come on,' he said, pretending to duck and dive and land punches in Keith's direction. 'Put 'em up! Go on, give it to me,' he urged, trying to look frightened as little Keith jabbed his tiny fists at Charlie's face.

'Come on, Keith, faster! Pow! Pow! Oh look at you! You're like James Cagney, you are. Come on, on me chin, lad – that's it.'

'Gocha, gotcha!' little Keith shouted, squealing with delight.

It was a good half hour before there was any sign of action from the house. Being out in the back garden, they had no way of knowing whether Nurse Emma had come or not, and that suited Charlie just fine. They'd know soon enough, because Margaret would come and tell them. Tell them and start barking her usual orders. Go get this. Go do that. Definitely don't do the other. And it would be like that for ruddy weeks, too. A new baby caused chaos and a terrible amount of noise. No, best to make the most of the peace while it lasted.

But it was Reggie who appeared out of the back door, rather than Margaret. He stood on the back step, looking ashen, and Charlie became worried.

'Where's nurse Emma?' Charlie asked him. 'Couldn't you find her?'

Reggie nodded backwards. 'In there. Urgh – but it's disgusting, Charlie. *Horrible*. Blood 'n' guts all over the place. Ugh!'

Charlie grinned and chucked Keith round the chin. It was his brother Reggie who needed toughening up. 'Shurrup, you sissy,' he said, 'before I set our Keith on you.'

Keith didn't need to be asked, crossing the yard and landing a punch on Reggie's thigh. And might have landed another, were they not interrupted by the unmistakable sound of a newborn baby's cry.

Charlie leaned in through the back door. 'Boy or girl, Margaret?' he shouted.

'Boy!' came the answer, followed by a long string of instructions.

That was that, then. A few weeks sleeping in the drawer beside his mam and dad's bed, then the little bleeder – whatever they decided to call him – would be in with the rest of them.

Great, Charlie thought, doing a quick calculation. That would be his share reduced to just a sixth.

Chapter 5

The war was beginning to make itself felt. Charlie remembered how, growing up, his mum had told him all about how certain groceries were rationed in the Great War, but now this one was under way it was still a shock to see how many things you couldn't get any more. And even the things you *could* get were strictly controlled – you had to buy them by producing a coupon from something called a ration book, coupons that were rationed in themselves. They were used to buy things that, when you could afford them at least, used to be plentiful: sugar, butter, tea, jam, meat, cheese and eggs. All gone – or as good as, because they were in such short supply. Charlie reckoned that Hitler, the horrible German leader who seemed to want to take over the world, must be trying to starve everyone into submission.

But, as Charlie had learned a long time ago, during the boxing match he'd won a shilling at, with desperation there usually came determination. And though he wasn't that desperate, he knew others were, and even those that weren't still had a hunger for the sort of basic things they'd once taken for granted.

Which meant opportunity.

Charlie had grown into a strapping hulk of a young man. To the astonishment of his mother (which always amused him) he now stood a good two or three inches over his father, and because he boxed at every opportunity he was strong, too. He'd also carved out a bit of a reputation for himself locally, and not just with the girls who swooned over him either. He'd lived on the Canterbury estate for less than a year now but already he was well known as someone you could rely on – or someone you didn't mess with, depending on your point of view.

Charlie was also independent, which mattered to him greatly. It had never really appealed to him, the idea of getting a job and working for someone else, and because he was clever and opportunistic, and had several ways of making a bob or two, so far he hadn't needed to, either. This too, despite his relative youth, had given him status in the community, and because of his size and strength most people would do anything Charlie 'suggested'. The local grocer, Theo Briggs, was no exception.

'So what I was thinking,' Charlie said to Theo one early autumn morning, 'was that I'll fetch you apples, plums and whatever else I get my hands on, and you keep it under the counter. It's up to you if you save it for them that's got coupons, but we'll split the income, how about that? I'll need to collect three-quarters of it, mind, Theo, because I've got my brothers to pay.'

Theo looked doubtful, which amused Charlie greatly. Balding, fat and in his forties, lending him an air of jolly respectability, it was no secret that Theo had been a bit of a rogue in his youth. In fact, local legend had it that he'd won the money to buy his shop in a card game – and that getting his winnings, apparently the loser's life savings, had involved a couple of bones being broken, too.

'It's illegal, Charlie,' he pointed out now. 'You know that.'

Charlie nodded his understanding, then placed both of his huge fists on the counter. Not as a threat – more as a form of persuasion, just as he'd seen old Mr Cappovanni do so many times over the years. 'I'll do it, obviously,' Theo added. 'But I'm risking getting caught, aren't I? Tell you what. How about we go halves?'

Again, Charlie nodded to convey his appreciation of Theo's position. Then he picked up an orange from a box on the counter. A rare and precious jewel now, oranges were only supposed to be sold to people who could prove they had children. And they came at a cost, too. He lifted it to his nose and sniffed it appreciatively.

'Lovely,' he said, tossing it in the air a couple of times. He then proceeded to peel it, throwing the bits of peel onto the floor as he did so. 'Tell you what,' he said. 'Like I said, I have my brothers to pay, don't I? And we're taking a risk of getting caught as well. So here's an idea. How about we don't go halves. How about we stick with three-quarters?' He looked down to the mess he'd created on the floor of Theo's shop. 'How about I also see to it that this place doesn't get turned over by all the starving little thieves on my estate? What d'you think? How about that?'

Theo shook Charlie's hand and the deal was sealed.

Charlie winked at his mam as he breezed back into the house the following morning, having finalised his plan overnight and strolled back down to Theo's again to get himself a hessian sack. Annie had little Malcolm on her hip and was sitting with Eunice, and by the expression on his sister's face Charlie reckoned they were having one of their regular discussions about Annie's wish for Eunice to leave school and go to work.

Eunice was 13 now, and Charlie knew she really didn't want to. She'd said as much to her more than once, and he reckoned she was right, too. She was a clever girl and if she wanted to learn more then she should do. After all – look at Margaret, who toiled such long hours as a machinist, putting her wages in the pot on the mantelpiece only to have them taken out again by her father, once his wages had run out. And it wasn't like they were going on anything useful for the kids, either. They were just funding his booze habit – helping no one, and often hurting them instead. He was still as free with his belt when he was drunk as he ever was. It was no wonder they'd recently found the pot smashed in the garden. No one had admitted to smashing it, but Charlie reckoned he knew. No, Eunice should stay put, to his mind.

It was a Saturday, which meant no school, which on a sunny day like this one meant his siblings would variously be scattered around the estate or, more usually, all together playing out back. There were so many of them now, they didn't really need anyone else for fun. They were like a tribe now, the Hudson kids, everyone said so. Well, except for Margaret, who'd started seeing some toff from down south. Called Bob Sloper, he'd come to Bradford to stay with an aunt, his mam and dad having been worried about him staying down in Kent since the bombings. He was joining up any day soon, so they'd be making the most of their last days together. And Margaret would be a right narky cow once he'd gone.

'Kids in the back garden, Mam?' he asked Annie now.

'They are, son,' she said. 'Can't you hear them? Our Reggie's got the tin bath off the hook and they've put some water in it to play in.' She shook her head. 'Been in and out all morning, our Brian and little Keith have. Little buggers, the pair of them. The ruddy floor's wet through!'

Charlie laughed as he went through the house and into the garden. She was right. There was a soggy trail of tiny footprints all over the lino, which he dodged as he made his way to the back door. 'Right,' he said, scanning his siblings. 'Reggie, Ronnie, Annie. Get your shoes on. And get your jumpers. You're coming with me.'

The kids stopped what they were doing and looked excitedly at Charlie. He knew they loved it when they were allowed to go on adventures with him. 'Me an' all, Charlie?' Annie asked him, as if not believing her luck.

'You as well, Annie,' he confirmed. 'You're eight now, aren't you?'

'Eight and a quarter,' she corrected. 'And why'd we need jumpers? It's boiling.'

She was a sharp one, was Annie, Charlie mused. She'd go far. 'Well, there you go, then,' he said. 'If you're already eight and a quarter you should be earning your keep. And as for the jumpers …' He tapped a finger against his nose.

'Yeah, but she's a *girl*,' Ronnie pointed out.

'Makes no difference,' Charlie told him. 'She's like a bleedin' boy, anyway.'

Annie puffed up with pride at this.

'Can I come too then?' June asked him hopefully. She was like Annie's shadow.

Charlie shook his head. 'Sorry, June. Too young for this one, I'm afraid. Besides, you gotta stay home and mind Brian and Keith, haven't you?'

Little Keith stamped his foot. 'I don't need minding!'

'Neither do I!' Brian agreed.

By this time, the older three had run inside to dry their feet and get their shoes and jumpers anyway. 'An' you best stuff some paper in them,' Charlie shouted after them. 'It's gonna be a long walk!'

*   *   *

Getting hold of sufficient clothing had always been an issue, but the war had made everything so much worse. The only time any of them got any extra clothes to wear was if Annie swapped one of her coupons for a pullover, or the odd pair of trousers. Everything was handed down, nothing was new, and nothing ever fit any of them properly. But they were so used to dressing like orphans out of some grim Dickens books that they didn't much notice, let alone mind.

Shoes were harder, though. Having holes in the soles was always an issue, and though in the drier months it could be addressed by the use of a little creative padding, come the winter Charlie knew it would be a different matter.

Right now, however, his three siblings couldn't care less. They were going on an adventure with Charlie and when he explained to them what it was they were going to be doing they were over the moon. It also became clear why they'd been invited along. 'It's cos we're small, isn't it?' Annie said, as they left the estate and began making their way across the fields. 'Cos we can wriggle into small spaces and you can't,' she said proudly.

'It's exactly that,' Charlie agreed. 'And it's a very important job. You've got to be quiet too, mind,' he added, anxious for them not to become too over-excited.

'So no giggling or screaming,' Reggie added, 'or you won't be coming again.'

It took around an hour to get to the place Charlie had already decided was the best option; what felt like miles and miles beyond the fields that abutted Canterbury, and further still, through other estates and unfamiliar streets. It was an area that had even Charlie momentarily short on chat, even though he'd already done a recce.

A suburb called Manningham, this part of Bradford felt like a completely foreign land, it was that different to what they knew. Consisting of wide avenues of huge houses, all of them three or four storeys high, it was the colour and brightness that was really arresting; with the sun shining down on lush flower-filled gardens and winking off fancy iron gates.

They clustered at the entrance of the walkway they'd emerged from. The houses round here ran in parallel streets, mostly, with pathways between blocks of houses at intervals. These led to a network of other, hidden pathways that ran along the backs of all the gardens. They were big gardens, too, and the pathways were usually empty, so it was from here that they could pinch the fruit unseen. 'Ooh!' Annie said, wide-eyed as she stared at the elegant homes around her, 'is this where the rich folk live?'

Reggie took his sister's hand and grinned. 'It sure is. Them in there,' Reggie said, pointing to the biggest of the houses, 'they're the rich baddies, and us, we're the outlaws who have to sneak in and take some of their fruit.'

'Like Robin Hood?' Annie asked.

Charlie laughed. 'Yes, Annie, *just* like Robin Hood. Only we're going to skip the bit about giving it to the poor and just concentrate on the robbin'.'

The older boys both stifled laughs at this. Then they each grabbed the hand of a smaller sibling, and led them round the backs, where, with any luck, there would be rich pickings for all.

Having checked there was no one around, Charlie was soon over the first wall. After which Reggie, who would remain stationed on the other side, passed first Ronnie and then Annie over. The next stage was for Charlie to simply lift the younger ones above his shoulders so that one could knock the fruit down for the other to collect on the jumpers they'd removed and placed on the grass near the wall.

They worked silently, swiftly and systematically. And by the time they'd covered half the houses Charlie had earmarked as possibilities, the sack was full to overflowing with apples. There were plums, too – even though a woman with a broom had chased them off, they'd managed to get away with an impressive haul.

They were chased some more, too, by a dog – thankfully only a small one – and by a man with a pink face and a bald shiny head, who'd come roaring from his house and only narrowly missed getting hold of Charlie's leg as he scaled the man's fence.

'You thieving little blighters!' he yelled, as the four of them scampered away. 'I'll be getting the police on the lot of you, just you wait!'

He'd have a job, Charlie thought, as they retraced their route back through the maze of pathways. They were lush and green, the scent of cow parsley hanging thickly in the air. But he made them keep running till they were a good mile away, before hauling the sack off his shoulders and letting them stop and get their breath back. 'What's a blighter?' Annie wanted to know as she munched on what was probably her sixth or seventh plum.

'Like a bleeder,' he said. 'But one who's going to have a bellyache come the morning.'

Charlie operated his fruit runs as often as he thought he could get away with it, widening his area of procurement with each new recce. He was making good money and he loved the way he was making it, not to mention loving being able to slip his mam a shilling here and there, for which she was always very grateful.

It didn't sit so well with his dad, though. He'd tried a couple of times, trying to offer him a few bob for a night out – making a contribution to the family finances, was how he saw it – but, now as ever, his dad never had anything good to say about it.

'Leave it on the shelf if you're giving it away,' he growled at Charlie one night. 'I suppose you think it makes you clever, does it? Well, it doesn't, lad, okay? Don't think I don't know where you get it from.'

Charlie balked at this. Like his father was so bleeding law-abiding himself? No, he wasn't – he just couldn't stand the thought of being in Charlie's debt. And knowing that was the way he saw it cut Charlie to the quick. But he didn't argue. He didn't dare. So he just left the money where he was told. But as he did so he vowed to himself that it would be the last time he ever gave his dad anything. Still, it gnawed at Charlie. Made him feel sickened and sad.

Did he really hate Charlie that much? It seemed so. And if that were so, then Charlie was done with trying to change his mind. In future, if he was inclined to share any of his spoils with anyone, it would be his mam and his brothers and sisters, and that was all.

The war might have been hard, but it gave as well as taking away, opening up all sorts of possibilities for making money, which Charlie was only too happy to exploit.

As well as fruit-picking, he found he also had a talent for ratting, a skill that was currently in great demand. Bradford was a mill town, first and foremost, its skyline punctured not only by the scores of factory chimneys, but also by the plumes of black smoke that spewed from them. And they were factories mostly built in another era, and the elderly buildings were riddled with rats.

Charlie had killed rats and mice since he was a kid, and not just to be useful, either. He killed vermin for fun. He loved to know he had the power to sneak up on them when others couldn't, upon which he'd usually batter them to death with a spade. Which again made him popular and much in demand locally, and as his reputation spread and he became known as 'Tucker Hudson, the Ratter' local factory bosses tracked him down and wanted to hire him.

The genius, as ever, was in the simplicity. Having agreed to quote for the job, Charlie would turn up and assess the extent of a factory's needs, then, having agreed a price, return to do the job itself. He'd come back prepared, carrying a box of the necessary equipment and poisons, which would be deployed only once the workers had safely gone and the factory was closed.

The box of poisons was, in fact, empty. Having the run of a place, unsupervised, Charlie would then proceed to fill it – helping himself to fabric remnants, knickers, sacks – whatever the factory produced, really – in quantities that were unlikely to be missed. He would then go on and kill just enough rats with his spade to ensure he had a sack full of dead vermin to show the bosses, before going on to sell his haul either in the pub or around the estate.

For all that he was thriving, however – what with his fruit runs, his ratting and, his main love, his boxing – Charlie still felt like he was living on borrowed time. They'd had one big air raid since moving into the house and it had really brought it home to him how real it was all becoming. As they crammed into the Anderson shelter – the family, and as many of the neighbours as could squeeze in – he realised it was probably only a matter of time before he was called up to fight for his country.

He wasn't afraid – he was afraid of nothing – and he also knew he'd be able to box, but it was an irritation he could do without. He liked being his own man. Doing what he liked, when he liked, and what he *didn't* like was the thought of being answerable to anyone else. His dad was the only fellow who had any say in what he did, and he didn't even like that. Not at all.

That late August night, as they'd taken cover from whatever the Germans were sending over, Reggie Snr – Big Reggie to his friends – had been drunk. Charlie could still visualise the scene – all the little ones scrabbling to get as close as possible to their mam, terrified by the sirens, terrified by the sound of shelling, terrified by the dark, terrified by the smell.

The adults did their best to lighten the atmosphere and chase the fears away for the children, belting out songs they still remembered from back in the last war, taught them by their own parents, in an impromptu sing-along.

Pack up your troubles in an old kit-bag,
And smile, smile, smile,
While you've a lucifer to light your fag,
Smile, boys, that's the style.

And it had helped, Charlie remembered, once everyone began joining in. Then, in all likelihood innocently, one of their neighbours asked Big Reggie if he'd seen action in the last war himself.

Reggie didn't even seem to try and come up with an answer. He just staggered to his feet – no mean feat in such a confined space – and in response felled the poor man with a single punch. But not for long – he was immediately back on his feet, and the entire shelter erupted in shrieks and cries and sobs as the two men went at each other, seemingly oblivious and refusing to give ground.

'He should mind his own bleeding business!' Annie shouted, as everyone else wanted to know what the heck had got into him. 'He couldn't fight the war, could he? He got signed off by the doctor because of his TB!'

Which was true, but not the whole truth, Charlie knew. Annie didn't know, but his gran had told him the real reason years back; yes, he'd been signed off, but it was nothing to do with having sustained lung damage as a baby. It had been a question of cash changing hands, pure and simple. He hadn't wanted to fight, so he'd paid the doctor to pronounce him unfit.

Still, this was his dad, and though he still very much had the upper hand, this wasn't fair on the nippers either, so he had a duty to step in. He stood up and stepped behind the hapless neighbour, placing an arm around his throat. He was called John Sheehan and lived a few doors away on the same street. A married man with two young kids, he'd always seemed all right to Charlie. Certainly didn't deserve what he'd just got. Even so, family loyalty had to prevail.

'Bleeding leave it, John,' he growled quietly, 'or you're a dead man, you get me? Surely you know better than to take the old bugger on.' He then dragged the man to the back of the shelter, sat him back down and then turned back to everyone else. There was a heavy silence, the children still clutching each other nervously and blinking in the gaslight.

'Come on, then, you lot!' roared Charlie, pointing upwards and laughing. 'Bloody Hitler could be outside, so let's sing him a lullaby, shall we? All together – *It's a long way to Tipperary, it's a long way to gooooo!*' And, in a matter of half a minute, they were back in full swing.

All except Reggie Snr, who was still too busy nursing his

pride. Should have fought then, Charlie thought. Simple as that.

The damage that night was the worst Bradford would suffer during the entire war. A bomb strike in the town centre had done extensive damage – including obliterating the huge Marks & Spencer building. Which was no accident, Charlie had told his mam a day or so later. It hadn't been one of the 'accidents' the papers would have them believing. It was strategic; the shop had been closed for the duration, in order to act as a storage facility for the surrounding mills.

'And the reason for that,' Charlie explained, having had his ear to the ground as usual, 'is because the mill storage facilities are being used for another purpose: to be made ready to house German prisoners of war. Mam, we have to face it,' Charlie continued as Annie sat there sobbing, 'I'm going to *have* to go and that's the end of it.'

'But do you have to?' she said, wiping her tears away with the corner of her pinny. It was such a familiar gesture – one he'd known his whole childhood. But he wasn't a child any longer. And neither did he want to be.

'Everyone's getting called up, Mam. Look, it won't go on for ever. And I'll send my wages home for you.' He grinned. 'That'll cheer you up.'

He got his papers and was gone before Christmas.

Chapter 6

Annie made her way through the estate, arm in arm with her new neighbour. Alice Donovan and her husband had recently moved in next door, their two sons having both been called up.

Annie liked Alice. She was as down to earth as they came, but quiet and unassuming. Her sons meant the world to her and Annie knew she was lost without them, and as a result Annie had sort of taken her under her wing.

It was a sunny day in May but the mood on the estate was anything but. The shortages were getting worse, and many were really living hand to mouth, her new friend included. So she was taking Alice down to the pop-up food shelter with her, determined to help her get something to eat.

'Are you sure I'm entitled?' Alice asked anxiously. 'Do I qualify, what with it just being me and Dennis?'

'I'm not certain,' Annie admitted. 'But I tell you what, love, I'll give 'em bloody hell if they knock you back. Your lads are off bleeding fighting, aren't they? That's left you as skint as the rest of us.' She quickened her step, fuelled by righteous indignation. It wasn't right to refuse Alice. It was her boys being gone that had left them struggling, wasn't it?

'Yes, but I don't have a houseful of other kids to feed, do I?' Alice answered. 'My Dennis said it's only for them that have big families. Just them and those that don't have a roof over their heads.'

'Well,' said Annie firmly, 'we'll see about that, won't we? It's not right, your boys fighting and you starving.'

And many more would have been starving if it hadn't been for the shelters, the Hudson family included. They'd been set up by the government in the poorest areas, and staffed with volunteers, who'd make soups and stews to distribute free of charge for those most in need; those who could prove they had many mouths to feed and not enough money to do so. These families were also awarded bread units. BUs, as they were known, could be exchanged for a loaf. It was a blessing for those like Annie and Reggie who really struggled, having so many kids, but people like Alice and Dennis didn't get them.

Annie pondered as they approached the shelter on the end of Ringwood Road. Chances were that, whatever she said, they'd turn Alice away. There were just too many people with loads of nippers who needed feeding, and she felt anxious that she might have given Alice unrealistic hope. 'Look,' she said, 'you just follow my lead and we'll give it a try, okay? And if they ask you outright, just lie. But if they don't give you any stew, you can have a bit of mine.'

'I'm not telling lies, Annie,' Alice said. 'And I'm not taking food that's rightfully yours, either. Not taking food off your little ones.'

'It's fine, honestly,' she said, looking at her friend's pinched expression. There was really nothing of her and she needed feeding up. 'They won't even notice,' she reassured her. 'I'll just water it down a bit. It'll be fine.' Though even as she said it she knew there'd be holy hell to pay if Reggie knew she was offering to give their food away.

'We'll be okay, Annie, love,' Alice persisted. 'My lads send home a bob or two when they can, at least.'

'Yes, but where does that go?' Annie countered, knowing the answer all too well. It went to Dennis, who probably drank half of it away, just like her own feckless husband did. *Men*, she thought. They were all the bleeding same.

There was no answer required to that one, and the two women exchanged wry smiles. 'It's okay,' Alice said. 'If I get nowt, then I get nowt. We'll manage. We usually do. And who knows? Maybe one of the lads'll send something soon. Speaking of which, have you heard from your Charlie lately?'

Annie pulled a face. That was a bit of a sore point. He'd been so full of promises to send his wages home, full of promises to write, but so far there hadn't been so much as a peep from him. He'd been gone six months now, doing his military training, no doubt enjoying the luxury of some warm cosy barracks, all the while knowing damn well how hard she'd be struggling without his contributions to the family pot.

'He's a *pillock*, Alice,' she said with a vehemence that shocked her. 'A bloody pillock! Hasn't sent us a bean so far, and probably won't either. Forgotten all about us, no doubt, the little twot.'

It was that – that sense of having been abandoned by her boy that stung the most. She missed him. Missed him dreadfully. In a way she couldn't really articulate, much less try to explain to Reggie, who'd have laughed in her face and told her not to be so wet. But Charlie had always been such a support to her; taking charge of his younger siblings, looking out for them in a way Reggie rarely did these days – he was either too busy working down the Punch Bowl or, much more likely, just sitting around drinking there instead. Just a single letter. That would do. Just so she knew he was thinking of them, at least.

The women arrived and took their place in the queue, the aroma of stew hitting her senses and making Annie lick her lips. She sniffed the air appreciatively. Might there even be meat in it? They hadn't had meat for a while now and she was craving it – though it would have been even longer if it hadn't been for Ronnie who, at ten, was shaping up to have his oldest brother's wits.

He'd run into the back room one afternoon and slapped a brown paper parcel on the table that was so big and heavy it made the table legs quiver. 'There you go, Mam,' he'd announced proudly. 'Take a look at that!'

'What on earth is it?' Annie had asked him, having only sent him out for dripping.

'Take a look!' Ronnie had told her, fairly bursting with excitement, and clearly unable to keep his secret a moment longer. 'I just thought it wouldn't hurt to try, so when I asked the butcher for the dripping I asked him if he also had a spare pig's head for our dog!'

'We don't have a bleeding dog,' Young Reggie'd said, as Annie opened up the package and found a pair of dead eyes staring up at her.

'I know,' Ronnie went on. 'An' the butcher knew an' all. But he laughed at me and said for my cheek I could have that one. I did well, didn't I, Mam?'

She'd told him he certainly had. And she'd cooked up such a lovely broth from that pig's head. Appropriately enough, the cheeks were the first things they ate, and Annie had made a lovely stew with the rest. It had lasted them almost the whole week.

But it was just a memory now. Today she'd be happy just to get to the front of the queue before the loaves had all gone.

'Morning, ladies!' a smiling man in an apron greeted them. Annie felt a rush of optimism. She'd never seen him before. That was good. He was holding a big ladle with which he stirred the contents of the giant saucepan in front of him. 'You brought your pans with you?'

Annie and Alice smiled back and placed the pans they were holding on top of the counter. Annie always brought the biggest one she owned – it would look less in there, she figured, which meant she might get the odd ladleful more. 'We certainly have,' Annie said, 'and before you go through the usual interrogation, we both live at the end of Ringwood, just up by the snicket. And I've 10 mouths to feed, an' she's got six.'

She held his gaze, with what she hoped looked like a world-weary air. If the mirror at home told the truth there was no doubt about it anyway. Without her make-up on, she bleeding looked like she'd had that many of them, an' all.

He cast his eyes back down to the pot. He clearly wasn't about to challenge her. Now all she needed was for Alice not to get an attack of conscience and confess. 'You wouldn't be telling me fibs, would you?' the man then asked, surprising her. But at least he had begun filling both their pots. 'Only I've had all sorts of nonsense this morning already. You wouldn't believe the number of little tykes I've had coming up telling me porkies – making out they live round here when I only saw them over at Manningham yesterday!'

Annie could have laughed, but she decided to take a different tack, just to be on the safe side. Make sure that, if he saw her again, he'd know she wasn't to be messed with. 'As God is my judge,' Annie huffed. 'And have you no shame? It's bad enough having to come here and beg off the bleeding government, without being treated like a criminal as well. And here's my BUs an' all. Or would you like to come back with me and do a head count?'

'All right, keep your hair on!' the man said, still scooping. 'No need for that, missus. I'm just doing my job. There you go,' he added, 'and there's a little bit extra for your trouble. Oh, and don't forget your loaf,' he added.

'See,' Annie whispered, as they headed home, carefully carrying their precious cargo. 'You've got a nice stew there, girl. Last you all week if you go careful.'

'Oh, Annie,' Alice said. 'I feel awful, I really do.'

'Awful? Whatever next! You need to wash your mouth out, Alice Donovan! You've got your boys off fighting for king and country, so that makes you as deserving as anyone, to my mind.'

'I won't say I'm not looking forward to this,' Alice admitted. Then she laughed. 'Six nippers? Perish the thought. I don't know how you do it, Annie, I really don't.'

Truth was, Annie really didn't know either. She knew as a Catholic girl she had to accept what the good Lord had deigned to give her, but frigging hell fire, her lot were more than just a gift, they never stopped! She sometimes wished that Reggie wasn't such a randy old bugger, because as far as she was concerned that was the only thing to stop her getting in the family way. Abstinence. And there was fat chance of that.

Still, there was nothing she could do about it. Though as they walked home in amiable silence, Annie pondered what Alice had said about her lads. It narked her that her big son hadn't sent anything home to her, yet he'd had the time to write to his hero, Mr bleeding Cappovanni. Oh, Cappovanni had passed on Charlie's best wishes – even said that he'd asked after the family and that they were to ask him if they needed anything off him. But no way was Annie going to do that. Reggie would bleeding kill her. It wasn't right. He should have written to *her*.

If things had been hard in the summer, Annie knew they'd only get worse in the winter. Not least because, contrary to what they'd been repeatedly told at the outset, the war didn't look as if it was going to end any time soon. France was now occupied by the Germans, there had been an air battle to end all air battles and London had been decimated by the Blitz.

Closer to home, talk was now all about the recent bombing of the city of Coventry, the pictures of which had been the talk of the estate; they had destroyed almost the entire city centre. Coventry was just two hours away by road and everyone was very frightened; how long before the Luftwaffe destroyed Bradford?

But though the fear was ever present, more preoccupying was the constant grinding poverty and endless struggle to try and make ends meet. And as Christmas approached it wasn't just food that was uppermost in Annie's mind; it was the impossibility of keeping the family warm, not least because they were constantly having to pawn things in order to raise sufficient money to buy any food.

One of their staples was Reggie's one suit, which, because his shifts at the Punch Bowl were all clustered between Thursday and Sunday, was invariably pawned for a few pennies every Monday morning. That would have to last them three days till he collected his wages, at which point they'd get it out again, ready for Reggie's next shift.

The pawn business was booming, and one person keen to exploit it was old Mr Cappovanni. Quick to see the possibilities to turn a profit once the war had begun, he'd opened a pawn shop on Canterbury front, the queues for which now often stretched way down the road.

It was a profitable extension to his already profitable local empire; another means to lend money at extortionate prices, together with a stock of saleable goods which he could pass on at a profit if the owners didn't pay up on time. People would pawn just about anything; their wedding rings were most popular and could get them a few bob, but Cappovanni would accept suits, clothing, coats, bedding, shoes – anything that others would pay good money for. And although it wasn't legal, he would also take ration books and bread units.

This narked Annie. She knew that if her Charlie were around he would be helping Cappovanni out in some way, and that would have meant that she'd have no need to take her own meagre belongings down to Cappo's Emporium. But needs must, and she figured that if she had to succumb to such things, she might as well make the best of it she could; it wasn't only Charlie who had an eye on a scam.

'Come here, son,' she said to Keith one early December afternoon. 'I need you to give me a hand, so I can get this parcel sorted, then we're off for a walk to Mr Cappovanni's.'

Keith, who was almost five now, jumped down from the big armchair where he'd been playing with some home-made paper aeroplanes. The other little ones were playing out in the back – even in this weather they wanted to be out – which was fine by Annie. Toughened them up for the months ahead. But little Keith was different; sometimes he just wanted to sit indoors and make things.

Keith was as fiery as his siblings – and just as keen on boxing as his brothers – but he also liked to 'use his loaf', as Reggie put it. He'd often spend hours, all on his own, engrossed in making something or other, often building himself quite intricate models using anything from scraps of paper to old shoe leather.

Perhaps she was being fanciful, but Annie secretly had lofty hopes for him; hoped that that good brain of his might take him far.

He dashed across to her now, the planes forgotten. Like all of them, he cherished time alone with his mam. 'Yes, mam!' he cried excitedly. 'An' will I get some spice?'

'We'll see,' Annie said, smiling at him, as he clambered up on to one of the chairs round the kitchen table. But the truth was she'd already decided he would. She was probably too soft, but all the kids knew that she'd usually buy them a little treat if she managed to get hold of a bit of money. Today she'd planned on buying some toffee apples to chop up if the morning's venture paid off. Which it should, she hoped, because bedding was big business now. All the pawn men loaned money on blankets, especially at this time of the year, with the harshest part of winter almost upon them. The problem was that Annie only owned two and they were both on her and Reggie's bed. And there was no way she could part with both of them.

So she had brought down the biggest, the scratchiest grey one, and now laid it out on the table, placing a piss-sodden army coat in the middle, along with some of the newspapers she had in a pile beside her. The coat was off the boys' bed and the air hummed as she began arranging it and stuffing newspaper here and there, but there was never any question of washing the stinking thing as there was no way they'd ever manage to get it dry again. But it would serve a purpose here, she knew, and after several rearrangements the coat and newspaper were completely hidden and she decided she was done.

'There,' she said to Keith, admiring her handiwork. 'One bale of blankets. Now then, little 'un, pass me the string and let's get this finished.'

He dutifully handed the ball of string over and Annie finished the job by tying up the bundle, with little Keith, who was almost as practised in this as she was, popping a finger in place each time so she could tie the knots.

'There we go,' she said as Keith took his tiny finger away from the last knot of string. 'Cappovanni will never know that's not actually four blankets, will he?' She tapped a finger to her nose and Keith giggled. 'Now we'll just wait for our Margaret to get home from work so she can mind the others, then me and you will go for a little walk, eh?'

She liked taking Keith when she went to Mr Cappovanni's. He was an impish little nipper and, just like her eldest boy used to do so well, he could charm the birds down from the trees. And though Mr Cappovanni was no pushover, he had a soft spot for Keith, who could chatter on for Britain, which meant he'd provide just enough distraction. He clambered down from his chair and jumped around in excitement. 'An' then we'll get some spice, Mam, eh?'

Annie nodded. 'Though no telling your dad, you hear?' He'd only give her hell, after all.

'I won't, I promise!' Keith assured her.

A little later, with Margaret home and the rest of the kids in safe hands, Annie and Keith joined the queue in the pawn shop. It was even colder now – the temperature going down with the weak winter sunshine – and she was glad that it had quietened down enough by now to ensure the line was only inside the shop. She watched and listened as the customers pleaded their case at the counter, some starting to cry when they got offered a pittance for things that were of so much personal value. It was humiliating, that was what it was, Annie thought, and she felt angry on their behalf.

It also made her doubly determined to play Mr Cappovanni at his own game. 'Here you are,' she said when they reached the front and Keith helped her place the huge bundle up on the counter. 'Four blankets there, Mr C. Me best ones as well, so don't be trying to give me peanuts for them, will you?'

Cappovanni grinned. 'Now, would I do that to you, Annie? Perish the thought. It's good to see you. And you too, lad,' he said to Keith, leaning over to chuck him under the chin. He then clicked his fingers and a lad who'd gone out back to put away the last client's things returned. Mr Cappovanni slid the package along the countertop towards him.

Annie sighed inwardly with relief as the boy picked it up and disappeared with it. For all her confidence with Keith, she never lost her anxiety that he might check it – that the next time might be the time when he undid it and exposed her, as she'd seen happen to others more than once. 'I hope you're all doing okay, love,' he said instead, and she thought he probably meant it. He and Charlie had been thick as thieves for such a long time, after all. 'And you know,' he added, leaning towards her now, 'as I told your Charlie before he left, if there's anything you need while he's away, you only have to ask.'

Annie'd wondered more than once if Mr Cappovanni might have a soft spot for her as well as Keith, even if he was old enough to be her father. 'We're doing okay, thanks for asking,' she said quickly, flashing a smile at him. 'Except, well, any chance of a shilling for them blankets? Only for a couple of weeks,' she added. 'Just till I'm back on my feet.'

'Make it half a crown,' a voice boomed from behind her. 'And I might even throw in a cuddle.'

She spun around, shocked to see her Charlie standing there, large as life, looking fit and well, with his arms flung wide open and a big canvas bag on the floor beside him.

'Charlie!' squealed Keith, crossing the space and launching himself at his brother, who scooped him up and twirled him around his head.

Annie pocketed the shilling that Cappovanni had already placed on the counter, then ran to give her son a hug as well. 'What are you doing back?' she said, while the three of them embraced. 'You sneaky little bleeder! You could have told us!'

'Then it wouldn't have been a surprise, would it?' Charlie replied, laughing. 'Anyway, here I am – "dishonourably discharged", as they call it. Spent a week in the clink –' he glanced over at Mr Cappovanni and grinned – 'and then they let me home. Seems I punched an officer and – ahem – not in the boxing ring, exactly. And they said they don't want my kind of riff-raff in the army.'

Cappovanni came out from behind the counter now and joined them to shake Charlie's hand, ignoring the subdued but clearly disgruntled queue behind them. 'Well, their loss is our gain, young fella,' he said, clapping his other hand against Charlie's back. 'Nice to have you back again. We've missed you.'

It was only on the walk home, Keith atop Charlie's shoulders, bag of toffee apples clutched in his hand, that it occurred to Annie that Charlie had gone round to Cappovanni's *before* going home, and that there seemed something not quite right about that. It should have been *her* seeing him first, shouldn't it? She was his mam – she was entitled. Not that crafty old rogue Charlie had always been so fond of.

But Annie was much too happy to have him home to even *think* about mentioning it. He was back. That was all that mattered. Things would be better now.

Chapter 7

1943

Charlie woke up and tried to gather his thoughts. The woman gently snoring by his side was a stunner – a real Marilyn Monroe lookalike, he decided – but he struggled to remember how he had ended up in bed with her. He eased himself from under the covers and swung his feet to the floor, trying to take in his surroundings. White walls and clean lino on the floor, decent blanket on the bed … There was even a sheet. He sighed as he leaned over to pull on his shoes. Only a prozzie could afford this standard of living. He wondered if he'd paid her.

'Morning, Tucker,' the girl whispered, reaching out a slim arm to stroke his back. 'You're not going already, are you?'

Charlie turned and flashed a melting smile at the pretty woman he couldn't even remember the name of. 'Sorry, gorgeous,' he said, 'but I've got work to do. Listen, do I owe you anything from last night, or did I already sort it?'

The woman pulled herself up in the bed and glared at him. Ah. So maybe he'd got things slightly wrong. She leaned to the side then and snatched up a pack of cigarettes.

Charlie stared in wonder even as he winced at what was probably coming next, seeing her in a completely different light now. She really *was* gorgeous, like a porcelain doll. Milky, almost translucent skin, white blonde hair and huge blue eyes.

He watched as she lit her fag and threw the box of matches across the room.

'Go on, fuck off, Tucker! You're as bad as they all say you are. Me? A fucking *prozzie*? You weren't calling me that last night, you big pig! You said I was special.'

She put the word 'special' in sarcastic finger quote marks and watched him pull his clothes on with disgust.

Charlie laughed out loud. A little spitfire this one was, and a mouth like a gutter rat to go with it. So she probably *was* a prostitute, then. Had to be; no decent lass spoke like that. He reached into his pocket and took out a two-bob bit, flicking it up with his fingers and catching it again.

'All right, all right, don't bite me head off, love! Look,' he said, placing the coin on the bedside table. 'I'll leave this anyway, just to say thanks.' He stood up then and, still laughing, retrieved his coat from the floor. 'It was a good night, as far as I can remember, and I *do* think you're special, you silly sod.'

He risked leaning down and kissing the top of the angry girl's head before nudging the coin towards her. 'I've got to go, though, so I'll probably see you around, eh?'

He only just dodged the ashtray as he ducked out of the bedroom door.

As he let himself out of the house Charlie did a final recce of the place and was impressed by what he saw. Tidy bird, tidy house – might be worth remembering this address for future reference, as – even better, he realised, once outside and able to get his bearings – it was only a five-minute walk from home.

Popping his hands into his pockets, he whistled as he strutted up the street, enjoying the feeling of the morning sunshine on his back and winking at every pretty girl he passed. Life was good. And would be even better if he could just remember the bird's name.

Trouble was, he couldn't. But perhaps that didn't matter that much, he decided. With almost all of the young men away fighting for king and country now, he practically had his pick of the local ladies, in any case.

'Where the bleedin' hell have you been?' Reggie barked, as Charlie let himself in. His father was sitting in 'his' chair and glaring over the top of the newspaper, the front page of which invited the women of Britain to 'come into our factories', just as his mam had told him had happened in the previous war. No chance of him doing that, though. Standing on a production line all day? No fear. He couldn't imagine anything more boring. Plus his talents, he knew, lay firmly elsewhere.

'I was out late, Dad,' he said mildly, 'so I thought I'd stay at our Margaret's.'

'Bleedin' liar,' Reggie growled as he rattled his paper. 'You're not too big for the bleeding belt, you know. You want to get yourself a real job. Pissing around for that Cappovanni again, and out on the ale every night. How the frigging hell do you think you're going to win any fights when you get into them states?'

Charlie reined himself in from pointing out the bleedin' obvious; that he *was* too big for a belting – he'd like to see his dad try it – that he wasn't 'pissing about' working for Mr Cappovanni, and that – actually – he had never lost a fight in his life.

Instead he racked his brains, still trying to remember where he'd been last night. It seemed like his dad already knew, which meant someone had been blabbing. But with the newspaper now firmly back in place, hiding Reggie's face, Charlie knew he had already been dismissed.

Knowing there'd be no point in answering back either, he went into the back to find his mam and get a pot of tea. The house was a lot quieter these days. Margaret had moved out to live with Bob's family in Listerhills until he got back from the war, after which they were going to move down south, to 'get away from all the shit', according to Margaret. Reggie had got himself a bird – Vera, apparently – and she obviously had her hooks in him because he was never home any more. As for the others, bar little Malcolm, they were all in work or school. So trust his mam to get herself pregnant again, he thought, as he entered the back room, with its comforting muddle of clutter and mismatched wooden chairs. It wouldn't be quieter for much longer.

She was placing a pan of water on the range, moving slowly and heavily, while his youngest brother sat playing with the tin soldier Ronnie had 'found' for him a couple of weeks back. Bless him, Charlie thought. It hadn't left his side since he'd been given it. 'Morning, Mam,' he said cheerfully. 'Enough in there for me?'

Annie straightened up and ran a hand across her huge stomach. 'Oh, you're back then,' she said. 'I hope she was worth it. That miserable get in there has been giving me hell cos you didn't come home.'

Charlie smiled at her. She only had a couple of weeks to go and then there'd be another mouth to feed. She looked knackered. 'Mam, what's he on about? What bleeding difference does it make to him? Anyway he's said his piece now, so that's an end to it. Now make us a cuppa, will you? I've got a mouth like a bleeding desert.'

Annie mashed a large pot of tea and reached for a rinsed-out jam jar to pour some out for him. 'Here you go, lad. Have this then go get a wash and a shave. I don't know where you were last night and I don't want to, either, but I'm sure you won't have had a wash this morning. And look at the time! What about your new job? What's happened to that?'

Christ, her an' all now. The pair of them, onto him all the time. 'Stop nagging, woman,' he snapped, feeling the effects of the ale now. 'It's my day off, so you can stop yer bleedin' mithering.'

The truth was that Charlie had been working at his job for a while now, and he could basically choose his own hours. If he fancied a day off, he could have one, no problem. Though the simple fact was that the more he was out there, the more he earned. And he *did* earn – more than his mam would ever know. But sometimes he *needed* a day off – especially days involving hangovers and nagging bleeding parents. He knew he'd only take it out on the punters otherwise; give them more than the usual bloody nose or broken rib.

No, Charlie wasn't 'pissing around' for Mr Cappovanni, as his dad put it. He was earning an honest bob, collecting money for him. Anyone locally who had taken out a loan or owed money for bets had learned – well, since Charlie had returned from his brief spell serving king and country – that if they didn't pay up what they owed, then they'd be getting an early morning visit.

A visit from Tucker Hudson was the last thing anyone wanted – not if they didn't have the means to pay. Just turned 20, Charlie had continued to grow right till the end of his teens and now he was a force to be reckoned with. A huge man, with hands like shovels, he could already knock a man out with a single punch, and he showed no favouritism to acquaintances and neighbours either. Didn't matter who it was – if anyone on the estate was late with their debts, they would feel the wrath of Cappovanni through his young protégé.

Charlie loved his job. And it suited him perfectly. It was actually a bit like training for a fight, really. He'd knock once at a door and, if it wasn't answered, he'd kick his way in and then hunt down the man of the house. A few slaps or a punch later and he'd be back out on the street, whistling as he pocketed the cash for Cappovanni. He got a cut out of everything he collected, so it paid to be persistent. Not to mention as violent as was necessary.

Not that his mam knew about that either. She'd have a dicky fit if he told her. No, there were some things mams were best off not knowing.

Charlie's mam didn't know much about his other job, either – which wasn't so much a job as another bit of entrepreneurship.

There were always opportunities to make a bit of extra money for yourself. It was just a question of working out what they might be. And Charlie had recently identified one such. Like many others on the estate he used the services of a door-knocker – had done since he'd begun working properly for Mr Cappovanni, because he wasn't a man who tolerated lateness.

Door-knockers had a particularly tedious job to do. In exchange for a few pennies per house, they got up before everybody else did, knocking up the breadwinner so they didn't oversleep.

The local door-knocker was a man called Stanley Sutcliffe. He'd been doing the rounds since Charlie could remember and he was clearly unhappy. He and his wife Gladys had six or seven kids to take care of, and Charlie knew he was getting pretty desperate. Charlie liked Stan; no matter how long it took, and whatever the weather, he would wait diligently by a door until it had been answered and he was sure the occupant would be up in time for work.

But paying Stan for his services was an entirely different matter – his pennies had been hard-earned and could be put to better use. So it seemed to Charlie that they could both do with a change in their fortunes, and he'd soon come up with a plan to achieve it.

As well as the morning door-knockers, there were also men employed as early evening lamplighters. Like the knocker-uppers, they would go around at a certain time every day, but in their case in early evening, to light all the gas lamps on the streets. This was a much better bet; a lucrative and much-sought-after job, as it was well paid (the lamplighters earned their wages from the corporation) and you didn't have to get up early to do it. There was also still time to get to the pub after work.

'You've got a face like a bulldog that's chewing a wasp, Stan,' Charlie said as he opened his door one morning and held out his two pennies. 'Had any luck getting another job sorted yet?'

'Not yet,' Stan replied. 'The wife's going mad an' all. Me working for a bleeding pittance.'

'You know what I've heard?' Charlie said, grinning. 'That there might be a position for a lamplighter coming up. What about if I see if I can get you a start on that as well?'

Stan's eyes widened. 'Really, son? You really think you could do that?'

'Well, no promises, obviously, but I can certainly do my best,' Charlie told him. 'Though in return, and for my trouble, there'll be no more charging me for knocking. How about that?'

Stanley shook Charlie's hand and agreed to his terms. He would have been daft to argue, and, anyway, it would just do him nicely – yes, he'd be working much longer hours, doing an early shift *and* a late shift, but it would provide the extra income he so badly needed. All that was left was for Charlie to put the next part of his plan into action, which he decided to do that very day.

Arthur Dixon was strolling down Tamar Street, just starting work for the night, when Charlie approached him. Within seconds – before he'd any idea what was going on, really – he was pinned up against the side of a house.

Charlie got straight to the point. 'Tonight, Arthur,' he said, 'you're throwing the towel in, buddy. A mate of mine needs this job and he's going to get it, you got that?' Charlie had one arm pressing into Arthur's gut and the other hand gripping his face. 'I said,' he repeated, 'have you *got* that?'

Arthur nodded immediately, eyes wide with fright. 'Okay, Tucker,' he burbled nervously, 'but what will *I* do? You got something else in mind for me, perhaps?'

Charlie felt sorry for Arthur, and understood his position. He was only in his mid-forties and had a crippled leg from polio. He'd never married, though, and without all those hungry mouths to feed it wasn't like he was desperate. He'd find something else. Charlie would keep his ear to the ground for him, too.

'Not yet, Art,' he said, 'but as soon as owt comes up I'll let you know, okay? Meantime, though, you have to jack it in. Tonight.'

Charlie released the unfortunate lamplighter and then smoothed down his overcoat lapels for him. He smiled at him then, almost apologetically. 'Nothing personal, you understand, Art. You *do* understand, don't you? There's just someone who needs it more than you do.'

The following week, Charlie answered the door to Stanley to find him with a big grin on his face. 'Thanks, Tucker, and

there'll be no more paying for this, pal. You just let me know if
there's owt else I can do an' all. Oh, and the missus says to tell
you she's really grateful.' He pulled a face then. *Really* grateful,'
he added, with evident feeling. 'Just found out there's another
nipper on the way.'

The latest Hudson nipper was on the way too – only in the case
of this one it was a question of hours rather than months. It was
barely a week after Charlie had put things in place for Stan
when it was a cry from his mam, rather than from his door-
knocker, that woke him. He winced as he heard the sound of
her animal wailing from the front room. It was a sound as familiar to him as that of a baby's cry – she must have gone into
labour with his newest baby brother or sister. He went downstairs, bleary-eyed, just as Eunice was pulling her coat on so she
could run and get the midwife. 'Go see to her, Charlie,' Eunice
yelled, 'and get one of the kids to nip round and tell Vera I'll
be late for work!'

Eunice had recently taken a job at a factory that made overalls. Reggie's girlfriend, Vera, had got her the start and they had
since become good friends. But that didn't mean *he* was, he
thought distractedly. Where did Vera live again?

He shouted this question after Eunice, who was now half out
the door. 'Ronnie knows,' she barked back, before shooting
down the path.

'Eunice!' he bellowed after her, conscious that his mam's
moans were escalating. 'Why don't *you* look after mam while *I*
go and get the midwife?'

She spun around irritably. 'Charlie, you're not even dressed!
Just get *on* with it, will you? Look after her, for God's sake!'

'Yes, but what am I supposed to *do*?' he shouted after her.
'And where's me dad?'

'In bed!' Eunice shouted as she ran down the street.

Shaking his head and feeling angry at his sister for leaving him to face his mother, Charlie closed the front door and went and peeped into the front room. Annie was on the lino, crouched down, with her back to the settee, groaning and rocking herself back and forth. Charlie winced. Her long skirt and pinny were up by her knees and her legs were alarmingly far apart. Charlie had witnessed this scene more times than he cared to remember, but never on his own, and never without a woman or two taking charge.

Annie glanced up at him, and her expression told him she felt exactly the same. That there were some things he was good for and there were some things he probably wasn't, and that this was definitely one of the latter kind. He felt suddenly very sorry for her. She looked terrible. He walked over and sat on the couch, putting a hand on her head and smoothing her damp hair from her forehead. 'You gonna be all right, Mam?' he asked her. 'Is the baby nearly here?'

Annie gave a weak smile before grunting in pain again. Then she surprised him by speaking in a clear, assertive voice. Once a mam, always a mam, he thought. 'I'm all right, Charlie,' she said. 'You don't have to sit here, lad. Go on. Go make us a big sup o' tea. The midwife'll be here in a minute.'

Relieved, Charlie gave her head a gentle pat and scuttled off into the back room, cursing his father for sleeping through it all as per usual. If indeed, he even *was* asleep, given his mam's groaning and wailing. He wouldn't put it past him to be up there wide awake but ignoring it, leaving everyone else – leaving *him* – to do what needed to be done. And that made him cross. His dad had put the wretched thing up there, after all.

He waited longer than perhaps he should have before going back to check on his mam – ostensibly because he was waiting for the pan of water to boil for the tea, but really because he was frightened that things might progress so quickly that he might be called in to help at the business end; not a place he ever wanted to be, not with his mam – not with *any* woman, for that matter – not under those circumstances, anyway.

But he was in luck. Eunice soon came bustling back into the house with Nurse Emma, and he relaxed a bit, deciding he would stay where he was till he heard the tell-tale scream that would signify the new addition to the family. He wondered vaguely whether it would be a boy or girl this time. Maybe a girl – they were currently outnumbered four to six – but, in truth, he didn't really much care. As far as he was concerned each new sprog meant one thing above all others – that he'd be expected to tip up even *more* of his wages.

He was just mashing the tea and remembering that he'd not woken Ronnie to have him run over to Vera's, when a scream came from his mother, followed by another from the new baby – so that was that – Hudson number 11 had been born. Now at last he *did* know what to do – take the tea in. He took some for his mam, who looked like she'd been hit by a lorry, as well as a pot each for Eunice and Nurse Emma. But not for his father.

Instead he went to the foot of the stairs, to wake the lazy old bugger up.

'DAD!' he roared, as loudly as he could.

Chapter 8

October 1950

Charlie staggered through the doorway of his 'two-up, two-down' terraced house at Buttershaw. Though he wasn't aware of much besides the thumping of his head, instinct told him he should be braced for a fight.

One thing he didn't need instinct to tell him was that he'd definitely been involved in at least one fight already. That much he *did* know for sure. He'd been in a boxing match down at Kings' Hall. Which he'd won – he remembered that much. Not that he even needed to – he'd never lost a fight yet. But what happened after that was all a bit of a blur. He looked down at himself as he attempted to close the door behind him quietly, and decided that perhaps it was better if it stayed that way. His jacket sleeve was torn, all the buttons were missing from his shirt and he seemed to be covered in a copious amount of blood. It was also morning – pretty early, too; dawn had not long broken – which probably meant he'd not been home since the day before.

And possibly longer. Through the fog came a vague stirring of memory. Had it just been the one night? Something told him it had been more, which made him wince as he made his unsteady way along the hall. He'd been at Yates's Wine Lodge, supping some Australian stuff, hadn't he? Yes, he remembered that much. But had that been just yesterday? No, he decided.

It hadn't. But he didn't really need to tax his brain further trying to work it out. As he entered the kitchen the answer was there right in front of him, in the expression on his wife Peggy's face.

It was also clear in the sight of the fat wooden rolling pin she was currently brandishing in her hand. She leapt from the chair she'd been sitting on, her eyes flashing. 'You bleeding dirty old man, Charlie Hudson!' she screamed at him. 'Two days! Two frigging *days* you've left me and these bleeding bairns to fend for ourselves! And look at the cut of you! You're good for nothing, you are!'

She swept the hand that held the rolling pin in a wide arc towards him and it was more luck than judgement that he managed to stop it connecting with the side of his head. 'Look at them!' she screamed again, pointing towards the fire. 'See them two, Charlie?' she added, raising the rolling pin again. 'They don't even know who you *are!*'

Charlie glanced towards the two babies currently cowering by the fire; little Russell, just two, and his not-quite-one sister, Dottie. Peggy was right. Even as Russell's eyes met his father's he began to howl, immediately setting off his sister, as if an enormous scary stranger had walked into the room. And Charlie, even through the fog, knew that it was because that was partly true. They certainly felt like strangers to him.

More to the point right now, though, was that he knew he was about to get another battering from his furious wife. He raised both arms to try and protect himself better, as the blows started raining down on his back and shoulders. 'Piss off, you silly mare!' he growled, but he knew it would make no difference, and he knew better than to try and stop her when she was in this kind of mood. So, partly cushioned by the booze, and at least knowing she couldn't keep it up for ever, he just stood and took the blows till she was spent. Only when her screeching had turned to sobbing did he risk making his escape.

'Get out of my way, woman, I need a piss,' he said, pushing past her to the hallway door.

This inflamed her all over again. She wasn't stupid, after all.

'Charlie Hudson, don't you *dare* take yourself off to bed!' she yelled at him. 'I mean it! I don't give a monkey's where you've been, you filthy bleeder, but you'd better have some money for these kids or I'll kill you. I *mean* it. I swear I'll bleeding *kill* you!'

She lifted the rolling pin again but Charlie could see that she had no fight left in her. In fact, she sat back down heavily on the chair she'd been sitting on when he'd entered, crying freely now, her keening mingling with the bleating of the children and the two little ones trying to scramble onto her lap.

'Of course there's money,' he said quietly, then, feeling bile rising in his throat, he hurried out of the kitchen, towards the stairs.

Peggy Hudson, she thought bitterly, as she gathered the children to her. *Mrs Peggy Hudson. Mrs Peggy bleeding Hudson.*

How fine that name had sounded once, even under the 'unfortunate' circumstances. How lucky she'd thought herself that the fabled Tucker Hudson had set his cap at someone like her. Had she been insane? The thought gripped her, as she tried to soothe her fractious infants. It had been a strange time indeed for her – just out of the Land Army, after doing her bit, no real sense of what the future held, but with a definite sense that perhaps nothing would ever be as much fun again. And there he'd been – so big and beautiful, such a catch. Everyone said so. Because everyone knew about Tucker Hudson – even more so, now he'd been making such a name for himself on the boxing circuit. To be on Chuck Hudson's arm had almost felt like being royalty.

Oh, she always knew about the drinking – that was the way it worked; that was the fight game. There was always the drinking, and she knew she could deal with it. She was a match for any man, wasn't she? She who'd been manhandling missiles and shells for the last two years. She'd soon show him who was boss when she needed to. And it was swings and roundabouts, wasn't it? No, he'd never been any sort of angel. But he'd been good to her, back then. She'd wanted for nothing and her girl-friends hadn't either. Peggy sighed heavily. That was all she seemed to do now. Cry and sigh. It had all felt so glamorous back then. So incredibly glamorous. But that was then. Not any more.

She leaned down and planted a kiss on each of her babies' heads. She could still smell the alcohol fumes that lingered in her husband's wake.

No, she thought. That was it now. Not any more.

He should never have done it, and that was an end to it. He shouldn't have listened to his mam – or his dad – all that 'make an honest woman of her' nonsense. He should never have agreed to get married, and that was all there was to it. It had been the biggest mistake of his life.

He grabbed the banister rail to steady himself and felt it move under the weight of him. His mam had been wrong. So, *so* wrong – that was now so bleeding obvious. On and on all the time about how it was important people saw he was respectable – on and on about how important it was that folk could see he was a 'family' man. Probably just wanted shut of him, now he thought back to it – make some room for the kids that kept coming, more like. Family man? *Him?* If only she knew! Last time he counted, him and Cappovanni had 24 prostitutes on their payroll – not to mention the four houses on Canterbury and two here on Buttershaw that they ran as illegal gambling dens.

Peggy was right about that, though. He didn't really know his kids at all. With the hours he worked, he thought, lurching fitfully upwards, his head spinning, was it any wonder? He hardly bleeding saw the pair of them, did he?

And as for her, no, she'd not been the ticket he'd thought she might be. Far from it. Oh, she'd been a right one before the kids came, no doubt about it. No, back then it was as if he could do no wrong. That soon stopped though. Once she'd got him. Got a bairn on her hip. A bairn he was out working to provide for! And then another, he thought irritably, as he pushed open the bedroom door.

No, he needed a woman like his mother, he decided; one who'd tend to his needs and not ask so many bloody questions. And as for the kids. He didn't *want* kids. That was God's honest truth. And she'd *known* that, he thought angrily as he tried to shuffle his feet out of his boots.

He managed one, before flopping down fully clothed on the muddle of sheets. He was fast asleep again in seconds.

It was dark when Charlie woke, the house still and cold and echoey, and, once again, he had no idea what time it was. Late at night? Early morning? His head seemed to suggest the latter. He felt like he'd slept for 24 hours straight.

He wrestled a tangle of blankets from his legs, and as he swung them to the floor he felt another sensation, as if he'd been boxing for 24 hours straight as well. There didn't seem to be a single part of him that didn't hurt in some way, from the back of his head, which felt almost too tender to touch, right down to his toes – still in the socks he'd put on God knew how long before – which felt comprehensively trampled.

Still, he thought, rising, and feeling the strength at least returned to him, if it was that bad it must have been pretty bloody good.

What he most needed now was a decent wash, however. A decent wash, a shave and a change of clothes. Then, since by his reckoning it was Sunday, he could spend the day at the pub, finding out what was what – well, once he'd faced Peggy, who'd be bound to be onto him. Nagging on about this and that and where he'd been and what he'd been up to, giving him more of the grief – of, course; *that* was why his head hurt – that he now remembered she'd been giving him when he'd come home. He sighed as he shrugged his shirt off. She was probably already down there lying in wait for him, ready. When was she ever bleeding not, these days?

Today, it seemed. It took no more than a cursory glance around to realise she'd taken the kids and left him. She'd left him before, of course – she was always stomping off back to her mother's – but this time he knew things were different. He took a second look. It wasn't that she'd taken everything, exactly. No, she'd left all sorts behind; stuff that was rightfully hers, too – not to mention the mantel clock her auntie had given them as a wedding present, and the silver picture frame containing a photograph of the two of them at the altar. He smiled grimly to himself. Probably no danger of her taking that.

No, it was the way of it – no shouting, no ranting, no recrimations, no note. No indication that she had the slightest interest in what he'd have to say about it, or even had a piece to say herself. She'd just quietly gone about the business of removing herself and the kids from his life. Permanently, just like she'd always threatened.

He walked back upstairs, wondering if he should feel worse than he did. Wondering if the lightness in his heart meant he lacked a soul. But the truth was that all he felt was a mild sense of guilt – but mostly for having done something he'd always known he shouldn't. Well, he'd certainly not be doing so again.

Once back in the bedroom, he looked around again, seeing it properly. He had no memory of what time it had been when he'd got in but she'd clearly been in here while he'd slept, and not woken him either. Just worked around him – the wardrobe was empty of her clothes and shoes and bags, and the dressing table of her usual clutter.

It was realising that which made him look for his jacket, knowing, even as he found it on a chair back (where he knew he wouldn't have put it), that when he pulled out his wallet it would be empty. And, of course, it was. He flipped it back and threw it down on the dressing table. So be it. He had no idea how much had even been in it, but however much it was she was welcome to it. He knew he owed her that.

As to whether she'd want more, well, that was fine too, he decided. He earned well, and he would very soon be earning even better. And his needs were few, anyway – always had been and always would be. As long as he could cover the basics of food, booze and clothing and – he smiled to himself – the occasional woman if he felt the urge, then he was fine. More than fine. He was dandy.

It took no more than an hour for him to wash, shave and make himself presentable, then, taking nothing from the house bar his trilby hat, suit and overcoat, he shut the door on his house and left for home.

It was a Sunday, just as Charlie had suspected. He knew because as he strolled the mile or so from Buttershaw to Canterbury he passed the church, and remembered what had woken him that morning – the bells ringing out, calling the good people of Bradford to come and praise the Lord. And it occurred to him now that the last time he'd set foot in the place had been for his and Peggy's wedding. Yes, thought Charlie, grimly, bloody St Joseph's had a lot to answer for. His family had kept them in business for years, what with all the weddings, funerals and all those bloody christenings.

How many now, all told? Too many. And forget the grand-kids and nieces and nephews – Charlie, by now, had 11 brothers and sisters – by anyone's standards, a lot. The latest brother, David, had been born four years previously, and along with him had come the pronouncement from Annie that, whatever Reggie might have to say about his conjugal rights, she was *not* having any more, and that was that.

Even with the older ones either courting or married off, it still left a house crammed with children, though; little David, Joe, Malcolm, Keith and Brian were all still crammed into a bedroom, while June – the only girl left – had the luxury of a room of her own. Which meant the sofa, Charlie mused as he nodded acknowledgement of several familiar faces and finally turned into their road. It was comfy enough after all, and why would he want the bother of looking after himself – and a house – when there was someone else willing to do all that for him?

It had taken Charlie all of five minutes to reach the decision that he would move back with his mam for a bit. It was the only sensible thing to do if Peggy had upped sticks perma-nently, after all, and every instinct told him she finally had.

Of course, moving back in with his mam also meant moving back in with his dad, which wasn't quite so appealing a pros-pect. But he'd long since stopped needing to worry that his dad would dare take his belt to him. No, he thought, running a hand over his freshly shaven chin, it was his mam who'd do her nut if she copped him looking bedraggled. He straightened his jacket lapels and opened the front door.

'Morning, all!' he boomed as he walked into the sitting room. 'Now, who's going make the prodigal son a sup of tea?'

Reggie, who was sitting in his usual spot in the best chair, looked over the top of his newspaper and grunted. He was in his fifties now, and a lot less in stature than he once was, but it was almost as if he could read Charlie's thoughts. And wanted to waste no time in correcting them, either. He might be the smaller man but he still held all the power. 'More like the bleeding bad penny,' he snapped. 'She left you then, finally?' He rattled his paper and went back to his reading then, clearly not expecting a reply.

'Nice to see you an' all, Dad,' Charlie said mildly as he shrugged off his overcoat. How had the old bugger worked that out already? He threw the coat across the back of the settee and sat down beside Joe and little David, who immediately clung to each other and scuttled as far away as they could get. 'What's up with you two nancy boys?' he asked them, bemused at their reaction. 'Frigging hell, mother,' he said to Annie, who'd now appeared in the back room doorway, 'what you been telling these two about me?' He leaned towards his youngest brothers and growled, 'Grrr, I'm the big, bad wolf!'

Joe and David yelped in unison and dived off the settee, taking cover in the space behind their dad's armchair while Annie, without saying anything, simply marched across the room and gave Charlie a clip around the back of his head. 'Leave 'em alone, you rotten sod. And if you're back home for a bit, you can go get some coal in before you make yourself cosy on my settee.'

She knew as well, then. Bad news obviously travelled like a blinking whippet. And Peggy probably broadcast it to all and sundry soon as she'd gone. Would have delighted in it in fact. Charlie stood up again. 'Make us a cuppa first, mam, and then I will. Where's the rest of the kids?'

'The lads are all out. And up to no good, I expect. And June's round our Ronnie and Jean's, helping out. Did you know Jean's expecting again?'

Charlie shook his head. Truth be told, he'd lost track of the goings-on of his many siblings and nieces and nephews. He couldn't even immediately bring to mind the name of Jean's first kid, let alone that she was in the family way again. He knew Jean herself, though. He'd never mention it either to his mam or his brother, but Ronnie's wife used to be a working girl. One of his.

Speaking of which, he thought, following his mam into the back room, how were she and his dad so apparently in the know about Peggy?

'How do you think?' Annie said to him when he explained what had happened. 'Was all round the estate by yesterday tea-time. I'm only surprised she put up with you this long,' she tutted.

Charlie could have said something in his defence, but decided against it. Whatever his mam said out loud, he knew exactly how she felt. Guilty, that was how, for making him marry Peggy in the first place. Made him do the 'right' thing knowing full well that it would turn out wrong in any case.

'But what about those bairns?' she said, pouring water into the teapot. 'You'll have lost them as well now, like as not.' She skewered him with a look. 'And you don't even care, either, do you?'

She turned away then, to get some tea, perhaps not wanting to hear him confirm it, and Charlie took the opportunity to hot foot it back into the front room and on to the safer ground of talking to his dad. He'd said his piece, and that would be the end of it, Charlie knew.

'So, father,' he said, sitting down as the little ones scampered off again. 'You still making a bob up at the Punch Bowl, then?'

Reggie snapped his newspaper closed and stared hard at Charlie. 'I am. You still making a bob fighting?' he asked him. 'Or have you given that up to concentrate on your mucky women?'

His father glared at him, which was all a bit rich, Charlie thought. Did he really think his son didn't know what he got up to? Where he sometimes went for a bit of comfort since Annie was having none of it? He had his needs, just like every other man.

Charlie returned his father's gaze, but said nothing. There was no point. Instead he shook his head sadly. 'Never satisfied, Dad, are you? Always got something to say. If you must know, they're fixing a fight for me at Blackpool next month. In the Tower, no less. What you got to say about *that*, then?'

Charlie'd been looking forward to telling his dad about the Blackpool fight ever since his head had cleared this morning and he'd remembered. And Reggie's response – a sarcastic snort – felt like a body blow. 'Bugger all, lad, bugger all,' he said, leaning back into his armchair. 'You go line Cappovanni's pockets if you like. Blackpool Tower, eh?' He chuckled unpleasantly. 'We'll see.'

Charlie felt his fists clenching almost automatically. Why hadn't he kept his sodding mouth shut? Why did he keep doing it? Thinking his dad might be impressed with *anything* he did? It was never going to happen and he should have known better. He was 27. When was he *ever* going to learn?

He stood up again and matched Reggie's glare with one of his own, though it was pointless. Reggie had already re-opened the paper, and was now back behind it, his son summarily dismissed. Decided, Charlie picked up his overcoat again. 'C'mon, Mam,' he said. 'Let's forget that tea, shall we? How about I take you out for a proper drink.'

Just as he'd suspected, his mam didn't need asking twice, and was already tugging at the strings of her pinny as she hurried back into the front room to pin up her hair. She didn't look in Reggie's direction and he made no move to stop her. 'Where we off to, son?' she asked. 'Local's not going to be open for a long while yet.'

'Cock and Bottle will let us in, Mam,' Charlie said. 'Now hurry up, will you?'

Now he'd had the idea he couldn't wait to get his lips round some ale. It would at least smooth out the hard edges of sleeping on the bleeding sofa. And more importantly get him away from the equally hard edges of his father's very evident disapproval.

Annie grabbed her coat. 'There's some stew in the pan, Reg,' she said finally. 'And our June'll be back to mind the little ones before it's time for you to leave – I'll pop in and tell her on our way,' she finished. 'Oh, and I'll come up to the Punch Bowl later on to meet you from work, okay?'

There was no reply, and his mam clearly didn't expect one. Neither did Charlie. He helped her on with her coat and led her outside.

'Miserable old get! Just ignore him,' Annie whispered once they were back out on the darkening street. She grinned up at him conspiratorially as she threaded an arm through his.

'Oh, I will,' Charlie said, glad there was one person who was happy to have him home. And he'd do better than that and all. He'd go and box at Blackpool Tower and he'd bloody show him.

Chapter 9

Keith couldn't remember ever having felt quite as excited in his life.

Well, not quite his life, but at least since the Christmas two years back when he and Malcolm had got a tommy gun to share when it was their turn to get a proper toy. They'd had hours and hours of fun with it, playing at cowboys and injuns, being soldiers, and James Cagney and John Wayne. It had lasted right through till the summer before it got broken, and even then they still played with it. But this was different. This was a completely different kind of excited.

He was older now, and was about to go on the adventure of his life. He was going to *Blackpool*, no less, so he needed to look as smart as could be.

And looking smart as could be was like a military exercise; one that had been many years in the perfecting, standing at this same kitchen sink, watching his brothers. *Blackpool*, he thought again, as he carefully placed the jar of sugar water at the edge of the sink. It was like something out of a dream. Or more a film – so he needed to look like a film star. And he would, soon as he could sort his flipping curls out.

His hair was the bane of his life, Keith decided, as he spat on the comb he'd pulled out of his back pocket and started dragging it through his thatch of waves. It was good that it was black, but why did there have to be so much of it? All heading off in different directions all the time, refusing to do as it was told.

He practised a devilish smile in the bit of mirror glass glued above the sink as he combed first one side into submission, then the other. That done, he took the front bit, which was flopped over his forehead, and fashioned it into a neat quiff. Last of all came the sugar water – the bit that made the difference – so he dipped the comb into it, then raked the back till it lay perfectly flat, near as good as. He then winked at his reflection before walking into the front room – slowly and carefully so as not to dislodge it – to find Annie.

'Mam, where's that lacquer stuff?' he asked. 'I need you to spray my head.'

Margaret had taken all the little ones to the pictures and Annie was making the most of peace and quiet, sitting reading Reggie's newspaper. She laughed as she put out her cigarette. 'Look at you!' she cooed. 'A proper little gent, aren't you? Blackpool won't know what hit it when my boys get there. Aww, Keith, though – do you have to flatten all your bleeding curls like that all the time? I like it so much better curly.'

Keith shook his head, albeit carefully, as Annie stood up and went over to fetch her hair lacquer – a tall red and yellow can that she kept on the shelf and which made everyone cough when she sprayed it. 'Course you do,' he observed. 'You're my mam, aren't you? It's a Jimmy Stewart, Mam. It's the fashion. *All* the kids have it like this. And what d'you think about this suit of our Brian's on me?' he added doubtfully. 'It's a bit big, isn't it?'

'What do I think? I think he'll bloody kill you if he knows you've took it, lad,' she said, grinning at him. 'So let's hope our Margaret's Bob comes for you before Brian gets back from putting your dad's bet on. Now, cover your eyes,' she commanded, as she prepared to unleash the lacquer. 'No, no, the suit looks fine, son. Now you've folded the cuffs and trouser legs up and everything, you look grand. Just the ticket. There. You're done.'

Satisfied that he looked the part now, Keith waited nervously by the front window, hoping Brian wouldn't beat Bob up the road. His brother wouldn't miss the suit exactly – at least, Keith didn't think so – but he'd have it off him in an instant, even so. Which would ruin everything. Ruin what was going to be the biggest adventure of his entire *life*.

'What d'you think our Charlie's doing right this minute?' he asked his mam. Charlie had left for Blackpool the previous day, with Mr Cappovanni, to get everything that needed to be organised organised. Annie smiled. 'I don't know,' she said. 'Not supping ale though, I hope! No, he'll be probably be limbering up for tonight's fight. Hey,' she added, going back into the back room to start on dinner, 'you just make sure and bring me back a stick of rock, okay? You're a lucky little bleeder you are, Keith Hudson.'

Keith didn't need telling. He couldn't believe his ears when Margaret's Bob had said he'd take him to the fight with him. Just him, and all – none of the others. Like he was special. Which he knew he kind of was because Margaret had told him. They liked doing the same thing, he and Margaret – things like reading and doing puzzles, and she let him help her with her crossword, which his dad never did. But for Bob to take him to Blackpool – that was really, *really* special, and he'd hardly been able to sleep a wink, he was so excited. He'd never left Bradford before, and he'd never dreamt that when he did, it would be to go to Blackpool. Everyone knew about Blackpool. It was really famous. Margaret had told him it was where all the rich folk went for their holidays. There was sea and sand and Sarsaparilla bars all along the sea front, and something called 'luminations', which he hadn't quite understood. All Keith knew was that he thanked God that Margaret had met Bob, because he was rich and as long as you behaved yourself properly he didn't mind spending his brass on you.

Bob had been in the war. And when he'd come out of the war he'd moved to Bradford for a bit, so that he and Margaret could save up enough money to buy a house down in a place called Kent, where Bob's family lived. Keith hoped it would be a while before that happened. Yes, he was used to his older family members going off to live away from home – Eunice and her husband, Ted, had already moved off to Lancashire to live on a farm – but that didn't really bother him like Bob going bothered him. He liked Bob and he wished they weren't going away. Bob was nice – and he wasn't afraid of speaking his mind, either, if the older ones picked on the younger ones. He'd clip them round the lug hole, just like he was their dad, and tell them to stop their nonsense and pack it in.

Let's hope if our Brian does get back first Bob isn't far behind him, Keith mused. It would definitely shorten the beating.

But it was Bob who came strolling up the street first. 'He's here, Mam!' Keith yelled as his brother-in-law approached the gate, hurrying back into the back room to check his hair one last time. Brian's shoes – the only good pair he owned – were already troubling him, too, and when he glanced down he could see there was a good inch gap between the back of his heel and the back of the shoe. 'Shall I stuff some paper in there, Mam?' he asked Annie. He couldn't wear his own shoes. He didn't want to be showing Bob up.

'Here', Annie said, balling up a couple of sheets of newspaper for him, 'stuff these in – let's hope your dad's finished his crossword, eh? And if he hasn't, too bad. You'll already be in Blackpool, won't you – living the high life! Aww, but I do wish you'd leave your lovely hair like it is.'

She was not quite his height – not these days, anyway – but she still went to ruffle the top of his head. He ducked out of the way just in time.

Blisters started up on Keith's heels almost as soon as they set off, but he ignored them. It was easy to ignore stuff when everything else was so exciting. He still couldn't believe that he was actually about to get on a train.

Not that he hadn't been down at Forster Square station many times, but that was usually with his brothers, to see if there was anything they could nick and sell on, or to offer to carry bags for the passengers, which would usually earn them a few pennies. But to be an actual *passenger*, actually getting on a train and going somewhere … Forget the blisters – he was so excited that he could hardly contain himself from jumping up and down.

Now he was here, he really *did* feel like a film star, and he couldn't wait to get sat down in a carriage. He'd seen train carriages when he'd snuck into the Gaumont to watch a matinée once, and wondered if there might be any Doris Day lookalikes travelling today.

'You about ready then, son?' Bob asked in his funny accent.

Keith grinned up at his brother-in-law. He loved the way he spoke. His mam told him it was cock-a-nee, which sounded funny in itself, but he was impressed he had an in-law who could speak it.

'I am, Bob,' Keith said as the train hissed to a halt in front of them. 'Ready to go watch our Charlie pummel the brains out of Walt Rivers!' He held up his fists and threw a punch in Bob's direction. 'Bam! Bam! And he's out!'

'Let's hope so, kidda,' Bob said as they stepped onto the train and he placed his brown paper package of supplies from

Margaret on the rack above his head. 'Let's hope so. Now, let me see … That's the way, sir – you sit there, by the window,' saying it like he was a butler or something, with a twinkle in his eye.

The train was everything Keith had hoped for and more. While Bob read his paper, he sat, nose to window pane, enchanted. Everything looked different when you saw it from a train. Places you knew became places you didn't know, and once they'd left the city it *all* became different, the buildings replaced by just miles and miles of countryside – field after field, like one enormous emerald blanket, with loads of little toy-town stations in between. This must be the green and pleasant land they sang in school about, Keith decided. It beat hanging around the estate *any* day.

There was more walking to be done again once they left the station over at Blackpool – they'd come all the way across England and it was beginning to get dark so they were off to get something called digs-for-the-night, where Bob explained they'd be able to sleep. 'But before we do that,' he said, 'we'll have a stroll down the prom like all the toffs do. Bet you've never seen the sea, have you, son?'

Keith shook his head, dizzy with all the questions going around in his mind. He was being bombarded with so many new sights and sounds and smells, and he wished time would slow down so he could take them all in.

'Yeah, but what are digs for-the-night, *exactly?*' he asked Bob as they strolled down a long road he said would take them to the sea.

Bob laughed his big laugh and Keith worried momentarily that he was going to try and ruffle his hair as well. But he didn't. He just clapped Keith on the shoulder as they walked. 'Just a place to put your head down, mate,' he explained.

'And what's a prom?'

Bob laughed again and swept his arm out to the left of him. 'That, my son, is the prom – short for prom-en-ade, since you asked – and if you squint a bit, you'll notice that over there is the sea. Can you smell it?' He sniffed the air appreciatively, and Keith did likewise. 'Come on, let's cross over and you can have a proper look.'

Keith looked and stared open-mouthed. Beautiful lights twinkled for what seemed like miles along a straight road that seemed to go on for ever. And as they crossed the tram lines, he at last saw the sea. 'Bloody hell, Bob,' he said, not quite believing he was so close to it. 'Is that an ocean?' It was such a lot of water – a huge mass that stretched as far as he could see.

'Is it hell an ocean, you daft beggar! It's just the sea. Come on though, son, it's four o'clock. We'll come back tomorrow for a proper walk. Right now we have to set about finding some pokey hole to rest up in.'

It turned out to be much more than that, though. Digs, Keith soon learned, weren't just beds you could sleep in. They weren't any kind of pokey hole, either. They were rooms you could rent in a massive mansion-type building, where lots of other people stayed as well. It must have been expensive, too, because he saw Bob pay the landlady using notes. And when she showed them the dining room, he felt like he was part of the Royal Family. Just wait till he told his mam about it all!

'You can help yourself to cornflakes and orange juice and toast over there,' she said pointing to a big cloth-covered table. 'And there's a full English, obviously.'

'Marvellous,' Bob said, in that confident, rich-person way he had. Keith could hardly speak for salivating at the thought of it. How the other half lived – what a result!

'Bit fancy, all this, ain't it, son?' Bob said, laughing, once they were in their room, as Keith flung himself on one of the two single beds, his anxiety about his quiff now entirely forgotten once he realised he had a whole bed to himself. 'Take your jacket off and get a bit of kip, why don't you?' Bob then commanded as he opened his package and set it on a side table. It contained a fresh shirt, a razor and a small bar of soap. Margaret always made sure Bob had everything he needed. That was why Bob always looked just right. He glanced at his watch. 'We've a couple of hours yet before we go to the Tower. We'll get a fish and chip supper on our way there, eh? How's that sound?'

Keith looked at the shirt and soap enviously, and wished he'd thought to ask his mam for a package just the same. But it didn't matter. Bob would probably lend him some of the soap anyway, and if he hung his shirt up when they got back it'd do just as well tomorrow. He lay back on the bed, feeling his hair all crackly from the sugar when it hit the pillow, stared at the ceiling – all swirls and whirls – and could not believe his luck. If he never had another happy day in his life it wouldn't matter. He'd never forget this. Not in a million years.

Chapter 10

'Bam!' yelled Keith, fists flying. 'Bam to the jaw! Bam!'

It was a few days after the boxing match in Blackpool, and he was in the back room sparring with Joe and little David. Charlie had reigned supreme, as Bob and Keith had expected, knocking out his opponent, Walt Rivers, in the fourth. Keith's memory of emerging with his victorious brother in front of a packed Blackpool Tower would be one he knew he'd cherish all his life.

He had been able to think about little else since, and when he wasn't talking about it, he was re-enacting it for his little brothers. He felt so proud he could almost burst, and if he hadn't had the boxing bug already he certainly had now.

'Bam,' he called to Joe again, dancing around him while little David clapped his hands excitedly, 'to the jaw, to the head, followed by a swift uppercut!' he chanted. 'Come on, lads, keep your guard up,' he added. 'Don't let me hit you or you'll never be like me an' our Charlie, will you?'

David swung his little arm back and landed a punch in his brother's belly. 'Like this, our Keith?' he said, grinning.

'Ouch!' Keith cried, doubling up and pretending to be in terrible pain. 'Tucker Hudson the midget strikes again! It's all over!' Which had both the boys jumping on top of him, giggling so hard that he had to remind them to keep the noise down or there'd be trouble.

It was supposed to be a school day, but Keith had overslept. And as no one else had got up to get the younger kids ready in his absence, he'd unofficially decided they could all have a day off. They were in the back room, him dressed but the little ones still in their underpants, because Charlie was home currently, and sleeping on the front-room sofa, and if they woke him he'd give them merry hell. Still, the back room was always the warmest place to be anyway, especially when someone remembered to keep the stove burning. It also provided a bit of light when the electricity was off, like it was today. Not that they didn't have any. They had a meter which had to be fed coins in order to keep the lights on, but Annie and Reggie rarely bothered about that, even in the winter, when it got dark really early.

'What's up with bleeding candles?' Reggie would ask irritably should any of them dare ask him about it. Then he'd launch into his usual sermon about how they were all soft, and how they managed fine with candles back when he was a boy. 'Wet between the ears, you lot!' he'd always finish.

And to an extent he was right, Keith thought, tickling his little brothers into submission. Though not in quite the way their dad thought. The opposite in fact. If you asked them, Keith reckoned, they wouldn't even know there was such a thing as electricity in the first place, it was put on so rarely. And there was so much else they didn't yet know about the world, and how it didn't all work quite the same as it did at home.

Only the week before, he'd come home to find his mam had been ranting on crossly about Joe's friend Tommy Herson, who lived across the road. Well, not him so much – it was his mam, who was apparently a 'snooty cow', and when Keith asked why, Annie'd told him it was because when Joe had been over to sleep there the night before he'd asked Tommy why there weren't any sleeves in their blankets. 'And did she go on about it!' Annie'd moaned. 'Couldn't wait to hurry across and have a laugh at my expense! And don't you *dare* laugh, Keith Hudson!' she'd railed at him, clipping his ear. 'Snotty cowbag!'

Today, however, she was fast asleep in bed, as was their father. Him because he'd been working the night before and needed to get some kip in, and their mam because she'd been up at the pub till really late, spending Reggie's wages as fast as he earned them.

'What's going on here, then?' came a voice. Keith turned round to see his brother Brian standing in the back room doorway, closely followed by Malcolm, who still looked half asleep. Not that Malcolm had needed to get up for school anyway. He'd been expelled now, for fighting, which he was always getting into trouble for, and now he was waiting to be sent to a detention centre.

Brian, on the other hand, was a good lad. Where Malcolm was considered difficult, due to his constant scrapping and fiery temper, Brian was the opposite. Unlike Malcolm, he didn't try to live up to his older brothers' reputations and had no desire to fight the world in order to prove himself. He just wanted a peaceful life, and though, like the rest of the Hudsons, he'd take whatever he needed whenever necessary, he wouldn't generally harm anyone in the process.

'We didn't bother with school,' Keith told the pair of them now, getting up off the floor.

'No school for us!' chanted Joe and David together.

Malcolm shrugged. 'Same as always.'

Brian did the same. 'Suits me fine,' he said. He was 15 now and only had a couple of months to go anyway. 'But why didn't our June get us up?'

Now it was Keith's turn to shrug. 'I don't know,' he said. 'She must have gone to work early or something.' June worked long hours now, because she'd got a job making cigarette cartons at a printing factory. She might have left as early as five. She often did. 'Anyway,' he said, 'now you're here, can you keep these two quiet for a bit? Make them some toast? I have to go round to our Margaret's.'

'What you off round there for?' Brian asked, eyeing him suspiciously. 'You're always at her house just lately, you little sneak. Or so *you* say. Who you *really* going to see?'

Keith grinned at his older brother and tucked his thumbs into his chest, then pulled his pair of imaginary braces back and forth. 'I'm off to see the wizard,' he sang, skipping past them, 'the wonderful Wizard of Oz …'

He dodged a kick from Brian and ran out of the house.

Technically, he wasn't even lying. He *was* going to Margaret's and he *was* going to see a wizard. Because Margaret's Bob was just like the Wizard of Oz in his eyes. Bob made things happen: since the Blackpool fight last month, he'd been doing just that. Seeing to it that Charlie made the most of all the offers that were now in the pipeline, including a bout set up for this very weekend. He was to fight an up-and-coming contender by the name of Micky Stenson, at the King's Hall, right here in Bradford. And best of all was that Bob had promised Keith that if he helped Margaret with the garden this week he would take him along with him to watch.

But, technically, he wasn't telling the truth either. Yes, he was going to Margaret's and he would be doing some gardening, but before that he had a bit of business to attend to, so Brian wasn't way off the mark.

He was off to meet his friend, Titch Williams, from over on Dawnay Road, who he was sure Brian would have referred to as his partner in crime. Not that what they were up to was really criminal, exactly. They were just doing what they needed to earn an honest bob. No crime in that.

It had been a job that had more or less fallen into their laps a few days earlier, when passing the new curry restaurant in Great Horton Road. It was something of a talking point locally. Since the war had ended, Bradford had been one of the cities that had seen a huge influx of immigrants, flocking from all over the colonies to fill the many industrial jobs created in the new market, mainly in the wool and textile trades.

This particular immigrant, however, had a different business in mind; introducing an exotic new foodstuff to the residents of Great and Little Horton. It was only a five-minute walk from Canterbury so the boys passed it often, but on this occasion they were not so much passing as sitting speculating, perched, as they were, on the wall by the sweet shop next door, sucking aniseed balls and practising how to wolf whistle just in case they saw Gloria Swan on their travels. Gloria was 15 and the current local beauty, which meant almost all the lads locally lusted after her, albeit fruitlessly, and Titch was particularly enamoured.

'She's been giving me the eye, Keith,' he said. 'No word of a lie. And I swear she was shaking her tits at me yesterday.'

Keith laughed as he popped another aniseed ball in his mouth. 'Has she hell as like,' he said. 'She wouldn't look twice at you, Titch. You really think she'd be interested in a 13-year-old like you? Besides, she goes out with Bobby Moran.'

Titch pulled a face and, in answer, stood up. He then rubbed a circle in the dust on the adjoining restaurant's window. 'I wonder what this place is like, Keith,' he pondered. 'You think the food's edible? My dad said they do curry and it's an Injun place.'

Keith joined him, rubbing the glass as well, and peering into the gloom. Then he jumped back. 'Come away, Titch! Look – the man who owns it is in there! I've heard he chases kids with a massive cleaver.'

'Does he hell as like!' Titch jeered, just at the moment the door opened, revealing an angry-looking man with what looked like a giant bandage wrapped round his head and a brown face.

'What are you boys bloody doing here?' he wanted to know. 'Causing me problems? I am sick of you boys coming round. Go on, piss off, you bloody kids!'

There was no meat cleaver in his hand, though, so Keith decided to be brave. 'We don't want no trouble, mister,' he told him. 'We wa' just looking in, that's all.' He pulled himself up to his fullest height, which was an encouraging almost-five-foot now. 'Actually,' he said, thinking on his feet, 'we were after a bit of work as it happens. Do you need any jobs doing? I've got a job on later but …' He wondered if he dared risk suggesting it. 'We could come back tomorrow and clean your windows.'

The man's eyes narrowed, but he evidently decided Keith wasn't being sarcastic. His shoulders relaxed a little, at any rate. 'What is your name, young man? And yours,' he added, letting his eyes run over Titch. 'I just might have something you can do.'

'Titch Williams,' Titch said proudly, 'and Keith here's brother is Chuck Hudson. The boxer,' he added. 'He's gonna be famous an' all.'

Trust him, Keith thought, glaring angrily at his friend. He hated it when people said things like that. Charlie had always told them to live off their own names, not his. He would go mad if he knew Titch Williams was bandying it about.

'And what's your name then, mister?' he asked the restaurant owner quickly. Though being foreign, he might not know who Charlie was in any case.

'Mr Abassi,' the man told them. 'And this …' he swept his arm across the front window proudly, 'is going to be best restaurant in Bradford, my friends.'

'Are you an Injun?' Titch asked.

'No, I'm not a bloody Indian,' he said with feeling. 'I'm Pakistani. I have come here from Karachi, with my family. So. You two boys want some work, then?'

Did they heck as like. And 15 minutes and some hard negotiations later, Keith and Titch spat on their hands and shook on what they considered a very lucrative deal indeed.

'We're gonna be rich! Rich, I tell ya!' Titch was singing as he ran down the street to meet Keith now for their assignation at St Luke's hospital on Little Horton Lane. He was wearing his trademark half-mast school trousers and an old army coat of his dad's.

'Come on, you daft pillock,' Keith said, laughing as his friend reached him. Titch and his family had even less than the Hudsons, but it was Titch's sisters Keith really felt sorry for. Being the youngest two of seven, they not only had to wear hand-me-down clothes – they had to wear boys' hand-me-down clothes as well, and had to play out in boys' trews and pullovers. No one seemed to much care, but Keith always wondered how he'd feel if he'd only had big sisters and had to do the same in reverse.

Keith pulled the pillowcase he'd brought out of his pocket. It was the only tool they needed for the job they'd agreed to do, which was to get as many pigeons as they could from the window ledges high up between the ward buildings, so that Mr Abassi could put them in his curry. Keith didn't know if pigeons would taste nice in curry, but he figured that what with everyone always saying that curry was really hot, it wouldn't much matter what meat was in it. And Titch was right – if they did well they would be rich, an' all. 'We'll get tons in here, won't we?' he said to Titch, shaking the pillowcase out.

'Yeah, but you're going to tear up them trousers good and proper,' Titch observed. 'Your mam'll kill you, mate.'

Keith shook his head. 'Don't care if she does. Anyway, they'll be fine long as I'm careful.'

And at tuppence a bird, Keith didn't care if they were shredded up or not. He'd just keep them out of his mam's way. And it would be easy work, too, he reckoned, as they made their way round the side of the hospital. They'd have the pillowcase filled in no time at all.

The part of St Luke's they were after was the space between two of the old ward buildings. Built close beside one another, they provided relatively sheltered window ledges to roost on and were handily just the right kind of distance apart that you could shimmy up between them, braced against the opposite walls, and get high enough to get to the birds.

It wasn't even hard. Pigeons were so dozy that all they had to do was grab them and quickly shove them under their jumpers, before shimmying back down, wringing their necks and popping them in the sack. There'd often be a bit of a commotion going on under their jumpers, but if they flapped about too much, that was no problem either. They'd just wring their necks where they were.

They got down to business quickly and quietly, taking turns to climb the walls and bag a bird. The space between them wasn't in a particularly exposed area, but there was always the chance there might be a security man on the prowl, so while one climbed, the other held the sack and acted as look-out. It didn't take too long. Less than a couple of hours and many bruises and grazes later, they had a bloodied pillowcase full of dead birds to show for their efforts. Titch tipped them out so they could count them – a whopping 12.

'Here,' Keith said, tossing an aniseed ball to Titch once he'd stuffed the lice-ridden bodies back in again. 'Plenty more where that came from once the Injun pays us!'

'He's not an Injun,' Titch corrected. 'Remember? He's a Pakistan man.' He popped the aniseed ball in his mouth with his scratched and filthy fingers. 'Twelve pigeons, eh? That's a shilling each!' he mumbled, speaking through it. 'I told you we were gonna be rich!'

And it did feel like riches, Keith decided, once Mr Abassi had paid them, and told them they could do exactly the same again for him next week. A shilling could buy you loads. Four pints of milk, a couple of beers or – much more important – enough sweets to last an entire weekend.

It would also be coveted by certain siblings and certain parents, so he stuffed it carefully down his sock, well away from prying eyes, then, while Titch went off to do some rag and boning with his dad, he ran round to Margaret's to make a start on the promised gardening.

Margaret's Bob arrived to pick Keith up Saturday tea-time as promised, and when he arrived Keith was glad to leave the house with him. His mum and dad were busy arguing – well, his dad was shouting at his mam, as per usual – because he had to go to work and she didn't want to stay in, which he kept yelling meant she was out spending his money even as he was earning it, and she was, as usual, giving him as much back.

It was the same every week and it had been the same way for ever, but though that meant it just went in one ear and out the other it was still annoying to have to listen to over and over again. Keith shook his head and tried to block out the noise as he promised himself that was no way on this earth he'd have as many kids as his own parents.

Today, he had better things to think about, in any case: seeing his brother knock seven bells out of the idiot man who had dared try his luck in the ring with him; a man from Leeds, Bob had told him, called Micky Stenson.

It seemed Bob wasn't anxious to hang around either. He and Margaret didn't have kids and their house was like a sanctuary. He must feel like he was going back in the war when he went in theirs, Keith thought. 'Everything all right in there, kid?' Bob asked as they got outside. 'Sounds like they're having another one of their barneys. It's no wonder your Margaret doesn't come round as much these days, is it?'

'Yeah, just the usual crap,' he said, seeing Bob's dismayed face. 'How many rounds before our Charlie will knock Stenson out, d'ya think?'

Bob laughed. 'Not very many, don't you worry, kid. From what I've heard, that Micky Stenson is a bit of a poof. Should be all over in three, I would have thought.'

Keith hoped so. He loved watching his eldest brother in the ring, but not for too long. He liked him to win early on. He knew he'd hate it if he had to sit there and watch Charlie go down. Not that that would happen in a million trillion years.

King's Hall, a majestic building that had been built in the 1800s, was one of the main Bradford city centre venues. With a seating capacity of 1,500, it was where the big stars of the day played, hosting big dance nights as well as major boxing and wrestling matches; where legendary fighters knocked seven bells out of each other. Tonight's bout wouldn't have any big names, unfortunately, but still there would be three or four up-and-coming fighters to watch – the big names of tomorrow, as Bob often said.

They'd arrived fairly early, but as they entered, through the enormous heavy wooden doors, Keith could see that the hall was already filling up. With groups of mostly men, but also the odd heavily made-up woman, and Keith was conscious of his relative lack of size and obvious youth. He ran a hand over his hair – almost all the men wore theirs slicked down and shiny, and he wished he'd plucked up enough courage to pinch some of his dad's hair grease. But the mood Reggie was in, he knew better than to risk it. If he caught so much as a whiff of it he'd have his belt off in seconds. No, on balance, Keith decided, he could live with his curls. Till he'd earned enough to get his own grease, that was.

Being on the early side, they found some seats close to the front, and Bob straightened out the order of ceremony sheet he took from his pocket. 'Our Charlie's on last tonight, son,' he told Keith. 'Hope you're not going to fall asleep before we even get to him.'

Keith couldn't imagine falling asleep in a million years. He'd happily stay awake all night if there was boxing to watch. 'No, it's good,' Keith said, the excitement beginning to build in his gut. 'It just means we get to stay longer.'

Bob grinned as he slipped the sheet back into his pocket. 'It does indeed,' he agreed. 'Hey, and budge up,' he added, waving at some men who'd appeared at the end of their aisle. 'Some of my mates,' he explained. 'Come to support our Charlie as well. You won't know them, lad. They're friends from the army.'

Keith duly shoved up to make room for Bob's friends, feeling proud as he ever did when Bob introduced him as Tucker Hudson, Chuck Hudson's kid brother.

'You box too?' one of them asked him. 'You going to follow in his footsteps?'

Keith felt too shy to say that but Bob answered for him. 'He's certainly got the moves,' he said, making Keith feel a glow of pride. 'Anyway, here we go,' he said. 'Support act's about to start.'

It felt like that, too, like they were saving the best till last, but that didn't take anything away from the excitement. The atmosphere was so electric it felt the very air was humming, and as the crowd yelled and jeered, oohed and ahhed and gasped in horror, Keith thought there wasn't a more exciting place to be on earth. Man against man. Nothing more. Just two men, fighting for victory. He felt like he could almost taste their blood in his own mouth, as they beat seven bells out of each other in the ring.

There was an interval before Charlie's fight – the big one – was due to start, and as everyone took the opportunity to go to the toilet, get drinks, or just talk through the fight before, he kept glancing at the back, hoping to get a glimpse of his brother. Where was he?

Bob nudged him. 'You wondering the same thing as I am, lad?' he asked him. 'Only Sid here –' he cocked a thumb towards one of his friends, a couple of seats down – 'says he's heard whisper he's been out on the piss all day.'

Keith felt a disappointed sigh escape him. He knew his brother liked a jar or six, but surely not? Not when this fight meant so much. He crossed his fingers automatically and hoped Bob wasn't right. This fight could open up all sorts of doors for his brother. There were trainers and promoters here from all over the place. The man sitting the other side of him had even pointed a couple out to him. He was about to say as much to Bob when the master of ceremonies started to talk into his big megaphone.

'Sooooo,' he said dramatically, 'Giant Chuck Hudson is a no-show, ladies and gentlemen ...' A surge of boos expressed the crowd's disapproval. 'And I'm told we have a bit of a challenge for you,' he continued over it. 'Do we by any chance have any boxers in tonight? Do we have ourselves a contennnnnnder?' A cheer rose now, the audience becoming animated, Charlie forgotten. Several clapped. 'Because Mickey Stenson,' the MC added, 'won't go home tonight without a fight, so which one of you fine young men would like to take him on?'

Keith almost choked when one of Bob's friends leapt up. 'Over here!' came a voice. A voice that was close by. 'Bob Sloper!' the man shouted. 'Bob Sloper will take him on!'

Keith's jaw dropped. It was one of Bob's friends! Bob himself went beetroot and tried to shrink in his seat. 'What the bloody hell are you on about?' he hissed to his mate. 'Are you *mad?* I'm not getting up there!'

Bob's friend – who seemed unlike any kind of friend, Keith decided – laughed and grabbed Bob under his armpit. 'Course you are, Bob!' he teased. 'You know you want to! I thought you said you were a bit of a face at the Thomas a Becket gym down south?'

Bob's other 'friends' all laughed out loud as he said this. 'It's all you ever bleedin' bragged about!' another one chipped in. 'Come on – time to show us what you can do, mate!'

Keith, powerless to do anything, and not sure if he even should, watched in astonishment as Bob was practically manhandled down to the front. It was true, he realised. Bob had said such things to him too. Many was a time he'd listened to his brother-in-law tell their Margaret how he could have been a boxer if only he'd kept it up. Well, bugger me, Keith thought, his non-appearing older brother forgotten, now he was going to have to pull it off.

* * *

Putting him in mind of his prediction at the start of the evening, Keith was at least pleased that it was mercifully quick. Quickest 'fight' he'd ever seen by a long chalk, he decided, as Bob, in less time than it had taken for them to announce the start of round 1, had had to be scraped from the canvas.

'I wasn't ready for him,' he kept saying, as they finally left King's Hall, his mates all joshing with him and ribbing him mercilessly. Keith was finding it hard to keep a straight face himself.

'Give over, Bob!' his mate said – the one who'd put him up there in the first place. 'He only hit you twice – bleeding *twice*! – and you lay down at his feet. *And* pretended to be comatose, you daft sod!'

'In fact, at one stage,' added Ernie, who was the biggest of Bob's friends, 'we thought you was kissing his feet, didn't we, lads?'

'I'd like to see you do it,' Bob huffed all the way home. 'And you mind me, lad,' he added, jabbing a finger in Keith's arm. 'Just you mind your tongue about this when you get home. I don't want it spread all over bleeding Bradford.'

And, of course, Keith promised. He felt a bit sorry for Bob, after all. He'd been brave to get up in the ring in the first place.

Even so, that was mostly because he knew he didn't need to worry. It would be all over 'bleeding Bradford' without him helping it along.

And it was. Charlie himself would delight in telling the tale for decades. How 'two-stroke Bob' was laid to waste in the King's Hall. It was almost as if he'd missed his fight on purpose.

Chapter II

1951

Much as Charlie loved his mother – and wanted to find a woman who was just like her – he was getting seriously fed up of living under her roof. No, he wasn't doing so all the time – he spent almost as much time at friends' houses, or those which were the working houses for the prostitutes – but he was becoming increasingly aware that, despite having his fingers burned with Peggy, he not only needed a permanent roof over his head but also a good woman to go with it.

Charlie wasn't short of admirers, either, any more than he'd ever been. And, at the age of 28, he knew he was in his prime now. Despite the odd hiccup – such as getting too drunk to turn up for the odd fight or two – he was still a very popular face on the boxing circuit. Huge and muscular, good looking and with a reputation as a winner, he had women from all over falling at his feet these days. He also had all the money he needed, courtesy of the now ageing Mr Cappovanni, but, in truth, he was bored out of his brains. Yes, the prostitutes served their purpose, but life was becoming more and more full of hassle; Mr Cappovanni, Charlie reckoned, must be losing his touch, because where once he could pay the police enough to keep them from nosing around in his business, now it seemed they were on him all the time. They were constantly sniffing around their 'houses of ill-repute', as the cops called them, and Charlie had found himself in court a few times lately. They'd even done a raid on one of the gambling dens.

No, Charlie decided, what he needed if he wanted to stay on top of his game was a quieter, more ordered, more gentlemanly life. Which meant getting a woman back into his life. But not just anyone; he didn't want one who'd take him on all the time, like Peggy had. He was after one who'd adore him in the same way his mam did – ask no questions, and give him a long leash to play with – not to mention the sort of comforts only an adoring wife could provide. The ones he definitely couldn't get from his mam.

Trouble was, where did you find one like that? They seemed increasingly thin on the ground.

It was a rainy Saturday in June. The sort of day when you couldn't defeat the weather. The sort of weather which meant that there was really no good reason why an evening in the Boy and Barrel should wait till the evening began.

Perhaps it was the day he was going to find the woman of his dreams, as well, because washed in with the squally showers and on a tide of chattering females there came a woman he didn't recognise but who immediately caught his eye. Petite, quietly dressed, very demure.

'Who's that?' he asked his brother Reggie as they waited for their drinks, nodding towards Reggie's wife Vera. Reggie turned to look. Vera was chatting to the group of women who had walked in, who were shaking out umbrellas and anxiously patting their hair.

'The blonde with the big bust,' Reggie asked, 'or the tall curvy redhead?'

'Neither,' Charlie said, shaking his head. 'Her standing behind the redhead. The little one with the brown hair.'

'Frig knows,' Reggie said. Then he nudged Charlie and winked. 'And if I don't know her, she's not worth knowing, if you know what I mean.'

Reggie headed over to their table with Vera's drink, but Charlie stayed where he was for a little longer, the better to observe the slender new girl in their midst. Reg was half-cut by now and, as usual, he was full of it; being the centre of attention as per usual.

And he was a lucky bugger, all told, Charlie decided, sipping his pint – given that he was married and already had two kids. Still, that was the thing with Vera. With a 26-year-old husband with the usual Hudson charm and good looks, she worked on a sensible principle – If you can't beat 'em, join 'em. So Reggie's Saturday afternoons out on the town still happened regularly, as did the non-stop female attention – whether Vera was there to police it or not.

But not everyone was hanging on his young brother's every word, Charlie noticed. The little one with the brown bob stood slightly apart from the others. In fact, if he wasn't reading things wrong, she seemed a little ill at ease.

Charlie bought another gill of bitter before walking across to join them, then, ignoring the rest of them, went straight to the mousy little thing he'd been watching and offered her the glass. 'Here you go, love,' he said, smiling at her. 'I noticed you didn't have a drink. Here, take it,' he urged. 'You a mate of our Vera's?'

She blushed furiously, stealing a glance at Charlie from beneath a sweep of dark lashes. 'Um, well, yes, I suppose I am. Well, what I mean is that I know her from work. She seems lovely,' she added quickly. 'And thank you for this.' She smiled shyly and held up her glass.

Charlie grinned as he clinked it, pleased with the effect he seemed to be having on her. 'You have a name then?' he asked her. 'I'm Charlie. Charlie Hudson, I'm Reggie's older brother.'

'Betty,' she said quietly, her cheeks still tinged pink. 'Betty Andrews. I think I've met you once before, come to think of it.'

'No, we've never met,' Charlie said, shaking his head. 'Trust me, love, I'd remember if we had.' Which had the blush spreading right across her face.

Charlie was mesmerised in moments. They found a seat towards the end of the increasingly rowdy group, started talking and didn't seem to be able to stop. It must have been a good 20 minutes before Charlie even realised that she'd barely touched her drink and she'd confessed that she didn't really like the taste of alcohol and, when pressed, said she'd have a bitter lemon instead.

They carried on where they'd left off then, the noise of the pub fading into insignificance all around them, and Charlie was glad Reggie was busy holding court with the other women; it meant that for the most part they were ignored.

And it was strange, he decided, listening to her soft, hesitant voice; women didn't usually have that sort of effect on him. Perhaps it was because they mostly talked too loud for him to hear them. With Betty he had to listen, and he could have carried on listening to her all night – it was something of a rude awakening when the landlord clanged his bell.

The next rude awakening was the arrival of his younger brother, lurching towards them, having broken away from the group.

He nodded towards the bar. 'Shall we go and give it to him, Charles?' he slurred, winking. 'Who does he think he is? Let's go put him straight about when it's time for us to go home, eh?'

Vera and her other friends had by now clustered around Reggie, laughing as they waited for the inevitable. Everyone knew how it worked in the Boy and Barrel; you didn't call time till Charlie had finished drinking.

'Go on, Chuck,' one of the women said. 'Put him straight!'

But Charlie didn't want to play tonight. In fact, he found himself wincing, something deep inside him seeming to know that him kicking off wouldn't impress Betty in the slightest. In fact, he felt sure it would put her off.

Surprised by himself – what strange, distracting thing was going on inside him? – he smiled at the little lady sitting so quietly beside him, then with a tight smile at his brother he shook his head. 'Not tonight, eh, Reg?' he said mildly but firmly. 'This little lady here is about ready for home and I'm going to see she gets there safely. How about you do the same for your Vera, eh?'

The group fell silent, all eyes now swivelling towards Betty, who was shrinking visibly in her seat. Not that she was a shrinking violet. Far from it, Charlie realised. She seemed an independent sort of lass – working because she wanted to rather than because she needed to. Charlie liked that. But neither was she showy. And having everyone gawping at her as if it was her fault he wanted to go home clearly wasn't on.

'You having a laugh?' Reg said finally, confirming it by glaring at Charlie and then narrowing his eyes at her. 'We're just getting started!'

Charlie covered Betty's tiny hand with his own, which dwarfed it. He stood up then, and, taking his lead, Betty followed suit. 'Not in here you're not, Reg,' he said. 'Come on, sup that beer.'

'Will I hell as like!' Reg retorted. 'I just told you, we've hardly started!'

'I said sup that,' Charlie said, moving closer to his brother. He had a good three or four inches on him. Always had. Not that it mattered. No matter how drunk Reg was, he wouldn't take his big brother on in a million years. Last time they'd scrapped – properly scrapped, properly angry – had been when they had been 19 and 17. It hadn't ended well.

'Walk your Vera and her silly mates home,' he said quietly. He didn't need to raise his voice. There was no need to shout here. 'I won't tell you again, mate,' he added. 'You get me?'

Vera stepped forward. 'Come on, Reggie,' she said nervously, holding up Reggie's jacket. 'I'm ready for the off now anyway. Come on. We'll get a take-away and go back for a bit of a party. Make the most of it while Mum's minding the nippers, eh?'

'Good idea,' said the landlord, who'd taken the prudent step of coming over to join them. The pub was almost emptied out now anyway. 'Take-aways, is it? What can I get you? Anything for you, Tucker?' he asked Charlie, smiling apologetically. 'I don't want no trouble – you know that. It's just my Irene. She's ready for popping the young 'un out any day now and she's knackered, God bless her.'

Charlie clapped him on the back. 'Then she needs her sleep, doesn't she?' he agreed, looking pointedly at Reggie. 'And like I say, this lady here needs her beauty sleep too, don't you? Well,' he added, seeing her smile and feeling a blush forming on his own cheeks. 'Need's not the right word in this case, obviously.'

She squeezed his hand. And it felt like coming home.

It was a three-mile walk to Manningham where Betty'd told him she lived, and Charlie thought back ruefully to his exploits robbing fruit from the gardens – might *her* garden be one they'd helped themselves from? It was the one topic of conversation he didn't intend broaching. Not that they seemed short on things to chat about. So much so that, despite the rain, Charlie he wished those three miles could have been 30. They walked arm in arm, hers nestled softly in the crook of his elbow, and continued the conversation they'd started back – oh – hours and hours ago now, swallowing up the miles without really noticing. He couldn't stop turning round and staring at her as they walked and talked. What the hell was wrong with him? Why the bleeding hell did he feel as nervous as she looked? He realised he'd never spent even a fraction of this amount of time continuously in a woman's company – did he and Peggy really talk about anything, ever? Talk had just been a prelude to sex, every time. And when not that, more often than not just a prelude to a row.

This was so different. She had things to say that he wanted to hear. About her current job, about her dreams of one day becoming a nurse and doing something useful with her life, about how different her life today probably was from his, with her being an only child and him being the oldest of so many. They even talked about Bradford City Football Club and how well they'd recently done against Southport. Charlie wasn't used to talking to women who had opinions on things like that. There was a kind of sparkle about her too. Her quiet air of confidence was captivating. This was a woman who wouldn't take any nonsense from a man. But something told Charlie that was because no one would ever give her any. And already – after less than a dozen hours in her company – he knew if anyone tried to, he'd want to kill them.

He left her at her gate, chancing a quick peck on the cheek before she hurried up the path to her front door, and waiting till she was safely over the threshold, loving the way her hair shone under the glow of the carriage lamp in the porch.

Ten steps back along the road and he was missing her already. He turned to wave, but she'd already closed the front door and turned the light off. He felt something stir inside him that was unfamiliar and rather scary. He was already counting the hours till he could see her again.

Chapter 12

Because Betty was a lady, Charlie treated her as such. For the first time in his life he found himself being one half of a proper courtship – which meant no sneaking her into one of his working girls' houses, and no fumbling around in the back alleys. She felt gentle as down and as fragile as a snowflake and he'd no more think of making a pass at her than fly to the moon. She was untouchable until he'd made an honest woman of her.

It was hard, though. Despite swearing that he'd never marry again, Charlie craved Betty. She was the polar opposite of Peggy, and that was a big part of her attraction. Softly spoken, delicate and feminine, she hung on to Charlie's every word. It was as if he'd stepped out of his old life and been dropped down into a new one; one in which nothing seemed to matter quite as much as making her happy.

The contrast with Charlie's regular life was a stark one, and it became clear early on that they were worlds that mustn't collide. He no longer visited his women, and sent his brothers to collect payments and drop them off at Cappovanni's. It was the same with the gambling money and collection of debts. Someone else did the running, and Charlie, ever mindful of the wagging tongues around him, discreetly collected his wedge once a week from the pawn shop.

Not that Betty seemed to want to ask questions anyway. She took him at face value – as a respected businessman who treated her like a princess, which was exactly the way Charlie liked it. Not to mention the way he needed it, because once he decided to put the past behind him and ask Peggy to marry him, there was someone else he was keen didn't ask questions as well.

With Betty's father Bart not being a Catholic like the Hudsons, there was no bar to the pair of them getting wed. And as Charlie wanted desperately to marry her (despite having sworn off it after Peggy) he needed to get him to agree to giving Charlie her hand; something that might prove challenging, to say the least.

Manningham was logistically only six or seven miles from the Canterbury estate, but socially and economically it was a world away, and Charlie still found it amusing to think he was now courting a lady from that very neck of the woods, and whose own garden might be one of the ones they'd robbed as kids.

It was a world of wealth and privilege, the world of not only businessmen (Betty's father owned his own spinning factory) but also of doctors, solicitors, accountants and judges, and Charlie was profoundly grateful that his notoriety had well-defined boundaries, because he knew that, if it didn't, he would almost certainly be judged himself.

Betty'd kept telling him not to worry; said her father wasn't the kind to make assumptions about people based on where they came from, and that he was very much looking forward to meeting him. And Charlie was sure she'd had a hand in that as well. For all her slightness of stature, when it came to what she wanted Charlie didn't doubt she'd have the strength of ten men. And, besides, Charlie kept telling himself as he kitted himself out in his best suit and brogues, how could Betty's parents not be decent, honest folk? They'd bred a princess, after all.

Not that they were going to make it *that* easy. 'I did have my concerns, I must admit, son,' Mr Andrews told him, as they sat together in a room that smelt of wax polish and flowers and Charlie had formally made his request.

Charlie blanched, but he didn't speak. Mr Andrews obviously hadn't finished yet.

'Yes,' he continued, 'when I heard what you did for a living, I must confess that my knee-jerk reaction was – I'll admit it – rather negative.'

Charlie's pulse began to race now. What had the man heard about him? He felt as if his heart might beat out of his chest. 'But then I realised,' Mr Andrews finished, with a wide welcoming smile, 'that you're something of a champion, aren't you, Charlie? A little bird tells me that you've never lost a round – is that right?'

Charlie was so relieved he couldn't quite manage to formulate an answer, and had to settle for a shrug and a nod of his head. The blush that coloured his cheeks, too, was genuine.

'And you know what occurred to me?' Mr Andrews said. 'That you're a winner, Charlie Hudson. And I like that in a man. And a winner is what my daughter deserves. A true champion in the sport of kings,' he said, gripping his huge hand to shake. 'So I'd be delighted to have you join the family, I really would.'

A winner, Betty's dad had called him. A champion at the sport of kings. If Charlie could have bottled those words and carried them home with him, he would have. He couldn't remember his father having *ever* called him that.

But Mr Andrews wasn't finished with him yet. 'You're a provider, Charlie Hudson,' he said, his eyes now glistening with what Charlie thought looked suspiciously like unshed tears. 'And I know she'll have everything she'll ever need. But one thing, lad,' he added. 'This is a day we've been anticipating all Elizabeth's life, as you can imagine. And we've been saving for it, too, so –' He stopped to clear his throat. 'If you'll allow me, I'd like to buy you both your first house.'

Charlie was touched – it was a gesture that had been completely unexpected, and he now had huge admiration for the man. But at the same time, it was never going to happen. Not only was Charlie never going to be persuaded to leave his part of Bradford, he was never going to be beholden to another man. It was a rule he'd decided upon a long time before. Around the last time his father had gone for him with his belt.

No, Charlie was a provider, as Betty's dad had just pointed out. And it was his firm intention to provide. 'That's very kind of you, Mr Andrews,' he said, 'but there's no need for that. I've already got the money to buy a house for us and get us started. In fact, I've already got my eye on one in Great Horton.'

'Oh, I see,' Mr Andrews said, clearly as thrown by Charlie's answer as Charlie had been by his generous offer. 'Well, that's up to you, my boy. Of course it is. But if you need any financial help, come to me –' he clapped his hand on Charlie's shoulder – 'and that's an order! Now, a drink to celebrate is what's in order now, I think, don't you?'

He winked at Charlie as he picked up a large crystal glass decanter from a tray on a polished table by the window. 'To good health and my Elizabeth,' he proclaimed as they clinked glasses. 'I know she'll be safe with you, Charlie.'

'I'd lay down my life for her, Mr Andrews,' he replied.

Chapter 13

December 1953

Charlie was besotted. There was no other word for it. Not only did he have the wife of his dreams in Betty, but now he had this perfect little princess as well. This perfect daughter that had only been a few weeks on the earth, and who he could already see was going to be as beautiful as her mother, however crumpled and red-faced she'd been when she'd arrived.

He gazed down at her, and offered her a little finger to hold on to, marvelling at the way her own impossibly tiny fingers gripped with the power of a vice. It stirred something in him that he couldn't quite articulate – and never would out loud, because he'd sound like the soppiest bugger on the planet. But he didn't need to. Betty knew. She'd said as much, over and over. 'Charlie Hudson,' she'd say, grinning at him, 'you're as daft as a brush, you.' Then she'd shake her head, but at the same time smile a contented little smile. And she was right. Baby Elizabeth hadn't stolen his heart. She'd just swelled it like it had never been swelled before. Swelled it so much that at times he felt it might burst out of his chest.

Not that he'd gone soft. Things had certainly changed since his marriage – he'd discovered how it felt to be properly happy, for one thing – but it was business as usual in all other respects. This all-consuming love might have melted him a little, but just as powerful was the protective rage that sometimes came over him, thinking that anyone might hurt her. And as he rocked his daughter now, he made a solemn and silent promise that he would kill anyone who ever tried to harm her.

Betty was napping on the sofa. It was a Thursday and she'd had a long and broken night nursing the baby, so when Charlie got up from where he was sitting, Elizabeth having drifted off to sleep, he was careful not to wake either of them.

He smiled as he noticed the sprig of mistletoe that had appeared in the doorway, dangling from a nail that had been bashed in. Betty must have put it there only recently, ready for Christmas. The big day was only three weeks away and she'd been thinking of little else. She had a childlike enthusiasm for everything to do with it, and this year, with a baby, she had gone into overdrive – making Charlie almost dizzy with her festive preparations.

Elizabeth needed to be put down in her cot, back upstairs, and on his way out of the room with her he paused under the sprig of hanging greenery, and placed a kiss on her fat little cheek. He then tiptoed upstairs with her, and placed her gently in her crib; a present from old Mr Cappovanni, who had made it himself, it was just about as beautiful a crib as either he or Betty could imagine, and set off by the beautiful bedding young Annie and June had sewn up for her, it really was a bed fit for a princess. He raised the sheet and tucked it in. All the while he had breath in his body, she and her mam would never have anything less.

Returning downstairs, Charlie stretched and looked out of the front window. It was bitter cold, with a heavy frost whitening the ground still, even though it was already mid-morning. And with both the main women in his life asleep, he decided it was high time he took a stroll over to the estate and paid a visit to the third one.

He'd hardly had a chance to catch up with his mam since Elizabeth had been born; what with keeping up with his business interests – which made no allowances for marital bliss at the best of times – he'd not really had time to draw breath. He felt stiff and lethargic from all the floor walking and night-time disturbances and recognised that what he most needed was to fix up a fight. It had been months since he'd last been in a boxing ring professionally, and though it would be a cold day in hell before he ever lost a match, he was conscious that he was 30 now, and with all those youngsters coming up, keen to try their hand at being the first to beat him, one thing he didn't want to have to do was work too hard for his prize money. No, he thought, reaching for his overcoat and scarf, he needed to speak to Cappovanni and see what he could get fixed up for the new year.

He then reached for his car keys – he'd recently bought a Renault which was the envy of all his friends and neighbours – but decided against. It was a good ten-minute walk from their cosy two-up, two-down in Great Horton. No, a nice walk would get the blood pumping in his muscles. Blowing a silent kiss at Betty, he quietly let himself out.

'Morning, mother! Morning, father!' Charlie boomed 15 minutes later, as he walked into the house and looked around. Given that school had broken up he'd expected the place to be crawling with kids and grandkids. Nothing had ever changed in that regard; the ones who'd left home and had their own kids seemed to send them round to his mam's to take their places. There was always the chance that Margaret's or Ronnie's kids would be round there, or young Reggie's boys. But the house was quiet. Almost as quiet as his own.

He found his parents in the back room, and Annie's face lit up in delight when she saw him, just like always. And, just like always, his dad barely acknowledged him. His only greeting was a grunt from behind his precious paper. 'Come on in, lad!' Annie said, coming round from behind where she was ironing at the table and beckoning him towards her for a hug. 'And how's our little Elizabeth?' She looked behind him towards the hall. 'Oh, love, you've not brought her?'

Charlie chuckled as he let her embrace him. 'Mam, I might be a lot of things, but do you *really* expect me to be seen out in public pushing a bleeding pram?'

'So why didn't you bring her in that fancy car of yours?' she said, clearly disappointed.

'Because she's asleep, and so's Betty, and they both need a bit of peace. Not being pawed over by all the nippers round here. Where is everyone, anyway?'

Annie laughed. She was in her fifties now and was beginning to look her age. But when she laughed it always seemed to knock years off her. 'Hark at you!' she chuckled. 'Proper little daddy, aren't you? And don't worry – no grandkids. Haven't you heard? Father Christmas is in town. Our Annie and June called round to take the little 'uns down to Busby's to try and get a glance of him. Boys are here, though.' She nodded towards the kitchen. 'Why don't you go in and get one of them to make you a pot of tea? And one for me and all while they're at it, tell them.'

'Will do,' Charlie said, flicking Reggie's newspaper as he passed him. 'You want a cuppa too, dad?'

'Not for me, lad,' his father said, finally lowering his paper and treating Charlie to a smile. Nothing ever changed. Even now he always felt he had to earn it in some way.

He went through to the kitchen to find his younger brothers, Keith, Joe and David, all warming their backsides by the old range. The contrast with his own home was striking. Where

Betty had the house decked out with paper-chains and sprigs of holly, round here you'd not even know it was Christmas. Since the girls had left home no one bothered any more. He was suddenly profoundly glad to have a daughter.

He nodded a greeting to his brothers, and pulled a chair out to sit on. With Brian having left home to join the RAF back in January, Keith, aged 16, was the oldest of them living at home now. Though he wasn't so old that he couldn't use a bit of big-brotherly direction, particularly since Malcolm had been sent away for a spell in an approved school to straighten him out. That wasn't Keith. Charlie was sure of it. He was a good kid at heart, but it had come to Charlie's attention that he'd been up to a bit of nonsense lately, and one of the reasons he was keen to come over for a catch-up was to have the chance to point out what needed to be pointed out.

'Now then,' he said, once they'd all gathered around him, 'you got yourself a job yet, young Tucker?'

It was strange how each of the boys became the next Tucker Hudson as soon as they started boxing. And now it was Keith's turn, Charlie mused affectionately, even with his sparrow's kneecaps muscles. He'd kept up the family tradition and was now getting a bit of a name for himself at the local boxing club in West Bowling. But that was just for fun. He wasn't about to become a prize-fighter.

'Nah,' Keith said, shaking his head. 'Not yet. But I've been doing all right. Earning a bob or two so I can give me mam some board and that.'

'So I've heard,' Charlie said, narrowing his eyes even though he was grinning. One thing they'd learned over the years – most of them, anyway – was that he always knew *exactly* what his brothers were up to, and Keith was no exception. 'You want to be careful, Keith, where you conduct your business, lad. Now

I don't much like a tea-leaf, as you know, but each to his own and all that. Just be careful not to shit on your own doorstep, you hear?'

Keith was immediately affronted, just as Charlie had expected. He was 16, after all, and Charlie remembered being 16. It would gall him to have his big brother poking his nose in his business. Which didn't mean he wasn't going to, even so.

'You mean the picture house? Leave it off, Charlie, we only took the scrap to sell!'

Charlie shook his head. 'I'm not on about the railings,' he clarified. 'I'm on about the stuff that's been going missing outside the Indian's shop. Don't think he doesn't know it was you cos he does,' he added, just as his little brother was about to protest. 'I've had to tell him I've given you a good hiding for that. And that's an end to it,' he added, as Keith, who probably thought he'd got away with it, hung his head. 'But no more thieving in your own backyard, you get me?'

He playfully punched Keith's arm, knowing that it *would* be an end to it. He *was* a good lad; just needed a little guidance along the way. 'So,' he said, sitting down by the range and turning to the younger ones, 'what have you little tykes been up to since I last saw you? How about you fill me in while our Keith gets me and me mam a pot of tea?'

'We've been doing good, Charlie, look!' little David said excitedly, shoving a foot shod in a newish-looking pump in his face. David was seven now and like a bottle of pop.

'They look grand,' Charlie agreed. 'How d'you come by them, then?'

'We've been up the playing field,' Joe explained. 'They had a big football league thing on – all the posh schools from out at Clayton and Manningham. Got ourselves kitted out good and proper.'

Charlie knew this was more out of necessity that simple thievery. There were rich pickings to be had in an empty changing room on those days; these were kids who not only had a full set of PE clothes – they even had spares, in case the set they had on in the morning got mucky. To kids who had nothing – or had to share a couple of ropey bits with various siblings as a matter of course – a couple of new items of kit felt like untold luxury. And what of it, Charlie thought. Those kids would hardly miss it, after all.

Which wasn't perhaps quite the case with car tyres. The other main 'business interest' the lads were currently pulling was to offer to protect people's cars at the very same sort of events. There were more cars than ever now, especially at the top end of society, and the truth was that, left unattended, they'd very likely be relieved of various items, either from the inside or – commonly – from the wheels. So, for the rock-bottom price of just a penny per car, the Hudson lads would protect a car till the owner returned to it, 'with our lives!' as they would always tell the punters.

And they did, too. Because, as night followed day, if the offer was declined, the owner would come back and find his motor up on bricks, with at least one tyre spirited away.

'We're earning loads,' little David told him. 'And we're not getting caught, neither, because we can all run really, really fast. You need some of our pennies?' he asked, having obviously just decided Charlie might have a need for some.

Charlie laughed out loud. 'Nah,' he said, ruffling David's curls. 'You keep your money, lad. You've earned it. Now where's that nice cup of tea, Keith? I'm parched.'

'And mine,' Annie said, bustling back into the kitchen with the iron. 'Oh, and I didn't tell you, did I, Charlie? Our Brian's coming home on leave before Christmas. Him and his mate

– that Gilbert he knocks about with? They've both got leave so they're home for Christmas.' She sighed happily. She was going to have her golden boy home again. 'Oh, it'll be so good to see our Brian again, won't it, Charlie? Feels like he's been away so long now.'

Charlie had his own views on that. He had nothing against his brother, but it did get a little tedious, all her 'our Brian' this, 'our Brian' that, all the time to the neighbours. He'd joined the bleedin' RAF, not the Royal Family. 'More mouths for you to feed then, Mam, more like,' Charlie said, winking at Keith as he took his jar of tea from him.

'Now't new there then,' Annie answered, obviously determined not to rise to it. 'And I'm sure we can stretch it. Oh, and something else. Our Reggie and Vera are going to have a Christmas party specially. Up at theirs. Just as soon as our Brian gets back. They're waiting specially. That'll be nice for him, won't it?'

Charlie raised his eyebrows. 'Yeah, you're right, Mother. It'll be just whoopy do for him.'

The other boys laughed. 'Whoopy do! Whoopy do!' Joe and David starting yelling, clasping each other's forearms and turning circles on the lino, before descending into what they were best at and fondest of – brawling on the floor.

'Go on, you two,' Annie snapped irritably. 'Piss off and scrap somewhere else! And *you*, Charlie, should know better. Our Vera said make sure you take that baby up to see her as well. Aww, won't it be nice, though? All of us together?'

Charlie sipped his scalding tea. Nice, but bloody noisy.

Chapter 14

Young Reggie and Vera lived up at Queensbury. Now 28, Reggie was in the building trade, and was doing well enough that they could afford to live in a more affluent area, in a little back-to-back terrace that he'd bought and done up beautifully, and which, second only to their boys, Colin and Barry, who were seven and four now, was Vera's pride and joy.

Their party was going to be the social event of the year. The whole family would be there; all the grandkids and cousins too, probably, plus as many friends as they could cram into their tiny living room, a quarter of which was taken up by Reggie's self-made, pub-style bar. He was the only one to have one and it was something of a centre-piece at a party, always fully stocked with booze and decorated with stolen brasses and studded panels.

'Will I wear my best frock, Charlie?' Betty asked, as they got ready for their evening out. She held up a dress Charlie had not seen her wearing in a long time – longish, lemon and white. Very summery.

'Won't you be cold?' he asked.

She smiled. 'At a party? I doubt it. Anyway, love,' she added, holding it up against her in front of the mirror. 'That's the least of my worries. I'm not sure I'll even be able to squeeze into it!'

Charlie grinned. 'You wear what you want, Betty, my love. It's only our Reggie's. Not a bloody palace.'

Betty turned around again. 'Oh but it's so *like* a little palace, Charlie, it really is. Your Vera has got good taste, that's for sure. By the way,' she added, 'will your Ronnie and Jean be coming tonight?"

Betty had finally been round to show off Elizabeth to Vera and had returned with more than just a warm glow of maternal pride. When it came to spreading gossip, Vera was the champion of the world, and Charlie knew full well what Betty really wanted to know. Would there be some sort of scene? Rumour had it that Ronnie's wife was playing the field a bit and Charlie had already told Reggie, in no uncertain terms, that Jean wouldn't be welcome tonight. He wasn't about to start having any arguments in front of his Betty. He knew how these things escalated, especially when they all got a few drinks inside them. There could end up being an out-and-out fight.

'Only Ronnie, love,' he told her. 'Jean can't make it. You know, with the kids and that. We're going to pick him up and take him in the car.'

Charlie's car wasn't only the envy of his friends, it was a serious status symbol within the family. Old Reggie had been dismissive, but then Charlie never expected any different when it came to his father, and when he'd brought it round the rest of them had bought it from the proceeds of his last boxing match and he felt very proud of himself – he was the first in the entire family to own a car.

'Will there be room, Charlie?' Betty asked. 'Aren't we already taking Annie and Brian?'

'And his mate Gilbert as well,' he confirmed, chuckling. 'I felt I ought to, given the rain.' He glanced out of the window. It was still coming down cats and dogs. 'But it's a big car, love, remember? We'll all squash in somehow, don't you worry.'

'Hmm, well,' Betty said, struggling with the zip on her dress. 'I suppose I'm going to be feeling squashed enough already, given the flippin' size of me still, so being squashed in a bit more won't make much difference.'

She was talking nonsense, of course, Charlie thought, and said so as well. And when she was done – kitted out in the best dress, which he reassured her didn't look too tight on her – she didn't just look fine. She looked radiant, especially when she had little Elizabeth in her arms. Even now he had to pinch himself sometimes that he'd got such a beautiful wife. Betty was not only beautiful on the outside, she was beautiful on the inside as well. She was the force in his life that made him want to be a better man; the reason he got up every morning. He couldn't quite believe it was possible to be this content. Having grown up with one very clear idea about how marriages tended to work, he was constantly astonished to find it didn't have to be like that.

He put an arm around her waist and kissed her cheek, having been warned off her freshly done lips on pain of death. 'You look the bee's knees, love,' he told her. 'And so does my little princess.'

There was no embargo on kissing his daughter so he did that now, as well. Betty had dressed her in a baby pink lace dress that young Annie had sewn up at work, and a knitted white cardigan that Betty's mam had made. He touched her cheek. 'Tonight, sweetheart, you are going to meet all your aunties and uncles. Let's hope they're all on their best behaviour for you, eh?'

Betty laughed. 'Come on, you daft sod,' she said, 'let's get going, shall we, or this little princess will have turned into Sleeping Beauty before we even get there.'

*   *   *

The party was in full swing when they all piled out of the car. They could hear the music blaring from out in the street.

'Frigging hell, Charlie!' young Annie moaned as she tried to smooth the wrinkles out of her frock. 'You know how to treat a lady, don't you? You squidge us up and then you blow a gale through the car for good measure. Why didn't you get one with the orange indicator thingies? I can't even feel my fingers any more!'

Brian laughed. 'You got any idea what they cost to buy, Annie? Bloody fortunes, that's what. One of our officers on the base has one. Hundreds of pounds it set him back, didn't it, Gilbert?'

'Oh, shut up your moaning, girl,' Charlie said. 'You got a free ride here, didn't you? You'd have a lot more you couldn't feel than just your fingers if you'd had to walk it. You'd be bleeding soaked. Anyway,' he huffed, 'I like doing my hand signals. Stupid new-fangled nonsense. If you ask me it's just another thing to go wrong. Oh, and another thing,' he said, locking the car doors and following the group in. 'A thank you wouldn't go amiss, either.'

Charlie could hear singing as he finally managed to cram into the tiny hallway. Keith, was his guess, and when he made it into the front room, it was confirmed. His little brother was perched on a stool singing a Frankie Laine song.

'Oh, that boy can chant, can't he?' his mam said when he reached her, her cheeks pink with ale and pride. 'What a voice.'

Keith was singing 'I Believe', and certainly holding everyone's attention – the women were all clapping along appreciatively, and the men swaying in time, and Charlie reckoned that if he didn't manage to make it as a boxer, he could make a pretty good living as a pub singer instead.

It wasn't long though before even charismatic young Keith was drowned out. With the drink flowing freely, it seemed everyone wanted a turn centre stage; well, in the case of the women, when they weren't cooing over baby Elizabeth, that was. Charlie had never realised how much joy you could feel just watching people admiring your baby. It was ridiculous; he'd had so little to do with it, after all. It was Betty who was the one who should really be feeling proud. But he couldn't help it, and, once he'd got a couple of beers down his neck, he gave Betty a break, doing the rounds with his tiny daughter in the crook of his arm, already knowing how many hearts she'd be breaking one day, and just hoping he'd still be around to see it happen.

'So it's hands off!' he joked to Brian's friend, Gilbert. 'I'm going to have a sign up outside the door.'

'Till when?' Gilbert joked. 'Till she's 40?'

Charlie laughed. 'I know someone's got to make an honest woman of her some day. Just need to be sure they're not anything like me!'

They roared with laughter at that, so much so that little Elizabeth started crying, and Betty hurried over to whisk her away and give her a feed. 'Well, I say me,' he finished, as Betty and Vera headed off up the stairs. 'I mean the *old* me. I'm a fine upstanding gent these days, of course.' Which made everyone roar with laughter even more.

The party was the great success they'd always known it would be. All those Hudsons in one place? How could it not be? Plus it was Christmas, after all. Annie and Reggie had left early, as they both had to be at work, but no one else seemed inclined to hurry, so it was long after midnight when it drew to a close and the guests began to make their way to their various homes.

And, it being the Hudsons, there was no danger of the neighbours kicking off at the racket as Charlie and the ones he'd brought piled, giggling, back into his car, pushing and shoving to get out of the icy rain.

'But don't you dare hoot that horn,' Betty warned him as she settled herself and baby Elizabeth into the front seat. 'Or I'll have your guts for garters, Charlie Hudson, you hear me?'

'And keep the frigging windows shut!' Annie added from where she was wedged into the back seat. 'It's pitch black and pouring and almost one in the morning, and no one gives a stuff about your wretched hand-signals, okay?'

Everyone stifled giggles at this, in deference to the sleeping baby Elizabeth, but it wasn't long before all thoughts of being quiet were forgotten, and as the condensation began to bloom on the inside of the car windows, so did the volume inside the car also increase. It had been a fun night, and, buoyed up by the promise of Christmas and the prospect of a day of rest, everyone seemed to have some anecdote they wanted to tell or felt a sudden urge to sing a bar or two of a favourite Christmas song.

Even Charlie, concentrating as he was on keeping the Renault in a reasonably straight line, joined in when Annie started singing 'I Saw Mammy Kissing Santa Claus'.

'Hey, Annie,' he called, above the din they were all making, 'can you imagine my dad if he caught our mam kissing Santa?'

'Jesus *Christ*, yes!' Annie spluttered, before noisily clearing her throat and beginning a passable impression (one of her favourite party tricks) of her bad-tempered father. 'You're a bleeding wicked woman, you are, Annie Hudson!' she growled.

'Now, now, kids,' Brian added, warming to the theme. 'That's it! Line up! You'd better choose, so help me God. Who's it gonna be? Come on! Me or Santa?!'

'You Hudsons,' Betty chuckled, having given up trying to soothe Elizabeth back to sleep. Instead she'd unswaddled her slightly and was jiggling her on her knee. 'You're blinking mad, you are! The lot of you! I never heard anything like it! I – whoah, Charlie!' she yelped then, as she was jolted against the door handle. 'What's happening? Easy on the gas, love. It's such a filthy night.'

'Yeah, Charlie,' added Ronnie. 'It's raining buckets out there. Go easy.'

But Charlie couldn't oblige. It was all he could do to keep control of the wheel. He didn't know why or how – he wasn't even sure where they were now – but the car had aquaplaned and suddenly lurched into an uncontrollable skid.

'Hang on!' he said, realising they were approaching St Enoch's bridge, and desperately trying to regain control of the steering. And to see – to make the road out through the lashing rain and condensation, but it was as if the car had a mind of its own now.

'Charlie! The wall!' Betty cried out as it loomed. Too late. The car ploughed into the brick and smashed through it even as she spoke.

They would be the last words he would ever hear her say.

Chapter 15

Keith shivered and pulled his coat closer around him. It wasn't his. Mr Cappovanni had lent them all heavy black overcoats for the funerals. It drowned him but at least it kept him warm.

It was the coldest, darkest Wednesday morning Keith could remember. The wind bitter cold, the ground crisp and uneven, the naked limbs of the trees that ringed Scholemoor Cemetery like the bars of an enormous prison cell. It was a week before Christmas – not that it mattered – but it was as if the birth of Christ had been forgotten. Barring a few odd sprigs of holly on a few frosted graves there was nothing here that gave any cause for celebration. He shivered under the greatcoat, feeling taut, like a spring. More than anything he wished he could run away.

The last few days had been a stomach-churning, terrifying blur; a nightmare that had started in the early hours of the morning, with a ferocious rat-a-tatting on the door. Then, as he stumbled down the stairs behind Malcolm and his parents, the policemen coming in, spilling into the front room, expressions grim and earnest, words coming out of their mouths like body blows. Bam! Brian dead. Bam! Betty dead. Bam! Baby Elizabeth dead. Bam! Brian's friend Gilbert dead too. Gilbert, who he'd met for that first – and now last – time, back in what now felt like a dream he couldn't return to. A dream that had given way to the crash of a chair hitting the lino – making him jump – as his mother had seemed to just fold up and sink to the floor, her face the colour of dirty dishwater, her hands

My Uncle Charlie

scrabbling for holds, her eyes staring up at him, wide with terror.

And then the crying. The soft muted weeping of the daytimes. Then the keening and wailing and howling of the nights. The sound that would wake him when his brain would let him sleep. Like an animal, it was. Like an animal caught in a trap. It was his own mother, but he'd never heard a sound quite so strange and terrible. It was frightening to listen to and he couldn't bear it.

Yet he'd borne it. Because what else was there for any of them to do? He'd been given his coat. He'd trudged the three miles to the cemetery. He'd sat through a funeral service, his eyes transfixed by the tiny white coffin that sat beside the larger, his ears trained on the same keening, gut-twisting sound that he knew so well, that had also come from Betty's mother's lips.

That had been the worst part, he decided. The bit that made his stomach clench. Seeing so many people in such obvious pain. And even though Betty's family had sat as far away from the Hudsons as they possibly could, it had still somehow felt like a union of grief. It didn't seem to matter that half of the congregation hated Charlie and the other half felt so sorry for him, they were in it together. It had been a strange, unsettling day.

And here they were again. All of them. Another enormous throng of people. So many people that they couldn't all fit into the chapel. To say farewell to his brother. The brother he still couldn't quite believe he'd never see again. And after today, the whole nightmare would be happening a third time. Tomorrow the chapel would be filled with Gilbert's family and friends.

But for Keith this was the last of it, and he was glad of that at least. An hour, he thought, glancing around the chapel, and they'd be done. So many people, he thought again, stunned by the numbers here for Brian. And at the centre of it, his broken, battered family. Ronnie – standing close by – with his head shaved and bandaged. His dad holding his mam up, because he dared not let her go. His brothers, all with faces white as monumental marble. His older sisters, weeping, being shored up by one another. Though no Annie. She'd be in hospital for months yet, his dad had told him. She'd broken her pelvis and her leg and she was going to need horrible-sounding procedures called bone grafts and skin grafts.

And no Charlie. *No Charlie*. Again.

Where, oh where had his brother disappeared to?

'I don't think he's coming,' he whispered to Margaret.

'No, love,' she said, placing a hand on his arm and squeezing it. She was grey as the sky and her cheeks were wet with tears. 'He won't be here,' she said softly. 'I think we all know that, don't we?'

And in her eyes was a thing that he'd not seen before. Not disgust, though he'd heard that so much since the crash. Not hate, like he'd seen burn in Betty's father's eyes. No, it was different. It was sadness, but it was mingled with pity. A kind of knowing pity that made his stomach churn all the more.

Where *was* Charlie?

More than anything, Keith wished he could run away.

Part Two

Chapter 16

August 1954

Charlie woke up and immediately knew where he was. He was lying on a concrete bed in a cell in Bolling Road Police Station – a place that was fast becoming such a familiar habitat that, had he been able to see straight, which was debatable at the moment, he'd be able to describe every inch of the stained, discoloured ceiling and count every strand of every single spider's web, like Robert the bleeding Bruce.

He pulled himself upright, taking time to let his pounding head resettle, flexing and unflexing his fingers as he did so. Had he decked anyone last night? If he had, they'd let him know. He swung his legs around next, letting his feet hit the floor, curling toes that had been encased inside the hot dampness of his boots for more hours now than he cared to remember. His mouth was dry. As was his hair – an exploratory rake through with his fingers told him he'd probably frighten the horses. But the suit he'd had on for the last couple of weeks now looked to be free of any tell-tale fresh splashes of blood. Well, as far as he could tell. It was getting that rank that it was beginning to be difficult to say. He stood and stretched, testing his limbs – no obvious broken bones, anyway – trying to recall what exactly he'd got locked up for.

He then walked the half dozen paces to the cell door. Time to let the coppers know he was awake.

'Come on, you bastards!' he yelled, banging on the door with his huge fists. 'Rise and shine! And you'd better come mob-handed if I'm not getting out of here today,' he continued, 'because I'm just in the mood for a good scrap!'

It took no more than a few seconds before he heard the sound of running footsteps. 'I'm coming, Charlie. Keep yer 'air on!' a young male voice called back.

Charlie recognised the policeman whose face appeared in the viewing panel in the door. It was a lad in his twenties called Constable Peek – a name that never failed to make him smile. He wasn't a bad lad, Peek, considering he was a copper.

Though he was still a copper. 'You're brave, lad,' Charlie said to him, laughing, as he stepped aside so that Peek could open the cell door. 'You come to take me on all on your own?'

Peek laughed nervously. 'No need for that, Charlie. I thought me and you were friends, weren't we?' He put a large key in the lock and opened the door, keeping a prudent distance. 'It's all right,' he said. 'They've told me I can let you go.'

Charlie raised his eyebrows. 'I didn't create that much bother then?' he asked. Despite the lack of physical evidence on his person, he felt sure he'd done something, but it was obviously lost in the alcohol haze. Just lately he'd been arrested more times than he could remember, and it usually meant a few days in the nick, not an overnight. 'Go on, then,' he said. 'What *did* I do?'

PC Peek took a step back as Charlie emerged from his cell, then went the whole hog and placed his hand over his mouth. Only now could Charlie see something he'd previously missed. He must have been so out of it that he'd pissed himself in the night.

Peek shrugged. 'No idea what you'd done before we picked you up,' he said, talking through his hand. 'We found you pissed and laid out in the middle of the road up Ivegate. Saw the blood –' he nodded towards the still unexplained splats on Charlie's suit jacket – 'and as we couldn't get any sense out of you we fetched you here for the night.' He removed his hand as he headed off down the corridor, Charlie following. 'You could have been robbed or set about if we'd have left you there.'

Charlie smiled as the constable went back behind his desk. 'Go on, then,' he said, 'let's get me signed out, Saint Peek. You've done your good deed for the week. And I'll tell you what – I'll try to remember to have a wash before my next visit at the weekend, eh?'

Constable Peek pushed a form in Charlie's direction. 'And pigs'll fly, will they, Charlie?' he said, handing him a pen.

Stepping outside into the bright sunlight of the early August morning, Charlie squinted and rubbed a hand across the stubble on his chin. He took off his jacket and decided he'd walk into town to pass a bit of time until the pubs opened. He jangled the money in his pocket and set off. The desk sergeant had just counted out his cash before returning it, so Charlie knew he had enough on him for a 'seer inner'. He'd sort out some more money when he'd had a drink and cleared his head a bit. He thought the Unicorn would be the best bet for early opening. Most of the town's drunks, prostitutes and pimps started off their day in there and the landlord would usually accommodate them at any hour. Chances were, he'd also be most likely to find a money source in the Unicorn too. Someone who maybe owed him a favour, or cash, and if not, certainly someone who wouldn't dare say no.

By the time he got to Ivegate, it was still too early for the pubs. It was Monday morning and on his way he'd passed people who were obviously going to work. Women in their pinafores rushing to get to the big department store, Busby's, blokes in their overalls making their way to the mills. Charlie had noted the looks of distaste as some had brushed by him and obviously noticed the state he was in. This hadn't bothered him in the least – in fact it was always amusing seeing them recoil when he growled and raised a fist at them. *Frigging insects*, Charlie thought, *scurrying around, getting in folk's way, just to earn a pittance for working all bleeding week.*

Work. The word hovered round the edges of his conscious-ness. As did Cappovanni, who kept talking about him 'finding his feet' and who a part of Charlie knew deserved better. But it was a part he couldn't seem to access right now. If he did it hurt so much he sometimes wished he could punch his own lights out. But he would drink, and the drink soothed the lacerating edges, and he could go somewhere far, far away from himself.

He needed a drink now. He peered through the large stained-glass window of the Unicorn, hoping to catch a glance of the landlord who would surely let him in, but couldn't see anyone knocking about. Hearing the town-hall clock strike, he realised it was still only ten o'clock so he took the weight off his throb-bing feet on the wooden bench just outside the pub. He eyed Yates's Wine Lodge opposite with suspicion. Had he been in there fighting the night before? A vague memory surfaced, but he couldn't seem to grasp it. Not that it mattered what he'd done – not from his point of view, anyway. He didn't care. He no longer cared about anything or anyone.

Just that drink. He licked his lips, feeling the familiar crav-ing. He was just about to get up and go and bang on the pub windows when he saw a face he recognised walking up the bottom of Ivegate. He squinted to get a better look, but knew he was right. It was Jean. Their Ronnie's wife. And someone else.

Mucky bint, he thought, his lips curling in anger now, automatically. She was tottering up the cobbles, arm in arm with Tommy Butler. The frigging coalman – and in broad bleeding daylight! And here, of all places, where she knew she might see him. Was she as stupid as she was dirty?

Charlie sat back on the bench and watched as they minced up the road, enjoying the moment when they stopped giggling at each other – like a pair of bleeding teenagers – long enough to realise just who they were walking towards. He stood up at precisely the moment when his sister-in-law's jaw dropped. Then he smiled. He towered over the coalman by a good eight inches, which could never fail to make him smile a little more.

'Tommy,' he said. 'Jean.' He nodded to each of them in turn. 'Fancy seeing you here. Doing a bit of shopping, are we?'

Tommy Butler was known for being a bit of a cocky prat and Charlie knew that even though he was scared half to death, he wouldn't bottle it in front of a woman. The sort of 'ladies' who went with him all thought he was such a great fellow – a hard man who could take any woman he wanted. Which just showed how little they knew. Oh, he took such delight in riding through the estates on his horse and cart, shouting 'Coal for hole!' in the hope that the local girls would oblige him by nipping out to give him a quickie in exchange for some free fuel. And sometimes they did and sometimes they didn't. And Charlie, who was very much of a live and let live mindset, might have even found it funny. There was no accounting for some women's taste, after all. Except for two things: that Tommy Butler had been sniffing around the wrong family and that Ronnie's Jean had thought it would be a good idea. On balance, he thought, had he not had other plans for the morning, he'd take just as much delight in pulling his fist back and slamming it into the hole in Tommy Butler's smug face.

Though he wasn't looking quite so smug now. 'Hello, Charlie,' he said, his smile as oily as his hair. 'I just bumped into your Jean at the bus stop.' He let go of her arm then and laughed like a girl. 'Silly bugger, she is – couldn't walk up Ivegate in them shoes, could she? Have you *seen* the bloody heels on them?'

Charlie looked pointedly at Jean. 'Silly bugger's about right,' he said, nodding. 'Eh, Jean? Fancy nipping into town in *that* sort of get-up. You know,' he said, skewering her on the end of a disgusted glare, 'you look *just* like I used to remember you. The way you looked when you used to work for me all them years back.'

Jean scowled at him, but her cheeks coloured even so. 'Say what you like, Charlie Hudson. I'm not doing owt wrong, am I?'

'Course you're not, Jean,' he said expansively. 'Tell me, where's them kids of yours? Our Ronnie minding 'em for you, is he?'

She lowered her eyes briefly but still couldn't stop herself squaring up to him. Once a working girl, he thought, always a working girl. Ronnie could've – *should've* – done so much better for himself.

And she knew it. 'What do you want, Charlie?' she snapped irritably. 'I've got to get on.'

Oh, I'll bet, Charlie thought. *Get on and work on your bleeding story.* 'I've just got out of the clink,' he said, matter of factly. 'And I need a few bob for a facer till I pick my money up from Cappovanni.'

They reacted as if they'd both been stung by wasps. Tommy Butler's hand flew straight to the pocket of his jacket, while

Jean plunged a hand into her bag. They both produced hand-fuls of coins simultaneously, which they plopped into Charlie's upturned hand. He could see Jean's look of distaste as the pennies left her hand.

'No problem at all, Charlie, mate,' Tommy said quickly. 'That should get you a few, and don't worry about paying it back or nowt. I'm all right.'

Charlie shoved the money into his own trouser pockets. 'Yeah, Tommy,' he said, 'You *are* all right. For now.' He then scowled at Jean and turned his back on the pair of them before sitting back down on the bench. He'd give them a count of five, he decided. No more than that. Five seconds to piss right off out of his sight or he'd be giving the cobbles a fresh coat of red paint.

He felt a stab of disappointment when he looked up to find they'd taken the hint and scarpered, and for a second or two thought he might just go after them anyway. He turned his hands palms up and scrutinised his fingers for a moment; a battered landscape of which every facet was familiar. He pulled them slowly inwards, imagining how satisfying it would be to drive one of them right into Butler's beaky face, and saw the filth that had accumulated under the fingernails. He could also feel the stiffness across his knuckles from the crusted layer of dirt. How long had it been since he'd had a bath now – a month?

Five seconds was being too generous, he decided, hauling himself unsteadily back onto his feet. He was sobering up, he realised. And with sobriety came demons. He needed to punch something badly, and Tommy Butler would have done nicely. But they were gone and he didn't have sufficient energy to go and find them. It would have to keep. Because right now he needed a drink.

And he needed it *now*. Not in half a bleeding hour. So he strode across the road and started banging on the window of the Unicorn with both fists.

He kept going till the landlord let him in.

Keith was leaning on the window-sill, watching out for Titch. It was tea-time and they were supposed to go out collecting scrap for a couple of hours, and hopefully helping themselves to a bit of lead, too. With any luck, once it was weighed in it would be enough to go and get drunk with.

He'd miss Titch, he realised, when he finally got his call-up for National Service. It would mark the end of something and he wasn't sure he was ready for the change. He'd definitely miss the larks they had together.

He saw him then – well, at least, he assumed so. There was certainly a wild-haired figure in the distance, staggering up the road, perhaps larking about or something, maybe dribbling a stone. His confusion was only momentary, however. There clearly wasn't any stone. Just thin air getting in the way, by the looks of it. And now it was obvious – the figure was at least a foot taller than Titch, maybe even more.

Then it hit him. 'Mam!' he called, suddenly animated. 'It's our Charlie!'

'*What?*' he heard his mam reply. 'What? *Here?*'

'On his way here, I think,' Keith told her as she joined him at the window, and pushed the makeshift curtain further out of the way. 'He looks like he's in a right state, as well.'

'Bleeding *hell*,' said Annie, sucking air in then exhaling loudly through her mouth. She'd been in the kitchen making Reggie some tea before he got home from work, but Keith knew all thoughts of food would have gone right out of her head.

Every other thought had gone out of his own head, for that matter. Charlie? Coming *here?* After all this time?

Keith felt suddenly fearful. He'd barely seen his eldest brother in months, and had no idea what to expect. Except that it probably wouldn't be good – he was still a good 50 feet away but they could already hear him.

Annie shook her head, as she wiped her hands on her pinny. 'Just look at him, bleeding swearing and carrying on at the top of his voice!'

'What's he come here for, d'you think, Mam?' Keith wanted to know, half of him wishing Titch would hurry up and appear too, the other half feeling pleased to at least see his brother, whatever kind of state he might be in. He'd only seen him twice since the crash, and both times he'd been asleep on a bench in the town centre, and in such a state that Keith had dared not approach him. His sister Margaret had summed it up when he'd told her. 'You did right, lad,' she'd said. 'He's always been a giant, but now he's an unpredictable giant. Best not stir him.' And Keith thought she was probably right.

'Why's he come here?' his mother snapped now, leaving the window to go to the door. 'For nothing, that's why, Keith! No, he'll have been fighting in town, got pissed, and forgotten he doesn't bleeding live here, that's what! Come on,' she said, beckoning to him. 'I'll need a hand.'

As far as Keith knew, Charlie hadn't really lived anywhere since the crash. Had never gone back to his house – not even once, or so his mam had told him anyway. Just left hospital and disappeared. Just the same as he'd left his house with Peggy. Only this time, his mam had told him, he'd taken the keys round to Betty's mam and dad. Just handed them over, told them they could have the house, and everything in it as well.

No one knew exactly what he'd been doing since then but they knew that mainly he'd lived on the streets of Bradford. Usually some bench in the town centre – the same one Keith had seen him on – but they'd heard tales that he just slept anywhere he collapsed and lay down after boozing all day.

'I'll bleeding kill 'em! Every one of 'em!' Charlie roared now, stumbling in through the front door and trying to focus, filling the space with an eye-watering stench.

'Sit down before you fall down, you silly prat!' Annie snapped, as he lumbered in and fell heavily onto the couch. Keith tried to shrink. The last thing he wanted to do was attract his brother's attention, not when he was in this kind of state.

Within moments, however, Charlie was flat out and snoring, and Keith ran across to help his mam tug at his boots. 'Here, Mam, I'll do it,' he said, bolder now he could see the state of Charlie. Forget throwing his weight around – he'd have trouble staying upright if he tried clipping anyone round the ear. 'Frigging hell, Mam!' he cried as one boot finally came off. 'Have you smelt that?' He held his nose and pointed at Charlie's stockinged foot.

Annie's nose wrinkled in disgust as the acrid smell hit her nostrils. But there was worse. As Keith leaned down to place the battered boot on the floor, he recoiled. 'Mam, I think he's shit himself!' he said, furiously fanning the air. 'You can't have him here like that, mam. Me dad'll go *mad*.'

'What else am I supposed to do?' Annie asked him, spreading her hands wide and sighing heavily. Her voice had gone funny, too. She was always like this when it came to Charlie these days. Keith looked down at his brother, trying hard to see what she saw. Where was the tall, handsome hero with the fearsome reputation? Now he just looked fearsome, at least to Keith.

'Well?' Annie asked again. 'What would *you* have me do? Throw him out on the street?' She shook her head. 'No. He'll have to stay and that's that. He's my son, and as long as there's breath in my body there'll be a place for him here. Your dad'll just have to live with it.'

Keith raised his eyebrows and walked back to the window, willing Titch to hurry himself up. One thing was for sure: no matter how mad his dad got, there was hardly any chance he'd say so to Charlie himself. Reggie hadn't uttered a word about his eldest since the day of the crash that killed Brian – not to him, as far as Keith knew, and not to anyone else either. It was as if his dad had decided Charlie was dead too.

But Keith also knew it was only a matter of time before something bad happened. Before Charlie, given the state of him, would come looking for a reaction, goad his dad into saying *something*, just the same as he always had. When that day came, Keith knew there would be hell to pay.

And it might just be today. So he didn't want to be around, just in case.

Chapter 17

Keith tiptoed soundlessly past his sleeping brother, shoes in hand, anxious not to wake him. Though how could anyone sleep for such a long time in one go? But it seemed Charlie could; he was still sprawled on the sofa, grunting and snoring, exactly as he'd been when Keith had returned from collecting scrap with Titch Williams the previous evening. The only difference, as far as Keith could see, anyway, was that the whole of downstairs smelt really rank.

He waited until he got into the back before putting his shoes on – given the state of him and the amount he'd had to drink, Charlie would no doubt be in a really foul mood when he did surface. The house was quiet. Joe and David had already gone to school and his mam was listening to the radio on the sideboard. It was playing very softly; seemed like she didn't want to wake Charlie either.

She stood up and placed the kettle on the swing-out slab that was attached to the range. 'You off to do some work for Joe, Keith?' she asked him hopefully, seeing his shoes.

Keith took whatever work came his way, because it was always so hard to find. As well as dabbling in the scrap-metal business, which paid okay but was thin on the ground, he sometimes worked as a painter and decorator for a local builder called Joe Laine, but never knew if he was going to be needed from one day to the next. He was hoping today would be a day when he needed him, especially with his brother currently sleeping off what looked like the bender to end all benders less than eight feet from where he was now.

Keith shrugged. 'Don't know yet,' he said. Then, seeing Annie's disappointed expression, he added, 'Don't moan, Mam. He pays me enough when I'm there, so the odd day off won't harm, will it? Where's me dad?'

'Where do you think?' Annie said, her expression changing to one of disgust. 'Still in his bleeding pit. Came home drunk as a lord, he did.' She shook her head and then tipped it slightly in the direction of the front room. ''It was a good job our Charlie was out for the count when he rolled in, or all hell would have broken loose.'

Keith followed her gaze. 'How long's he staying?'

Annie pursed her lips. 'Now don't you start. He'll be here as long as he's here, and that's that.'

Keith laced his shoes as his mam poured hot water over some already used tea leaves and then set the jar aside to mash. He *definitely* hoped Joe Laine needed him today now. He knew his dad would get up in a foul mood on account of Charlie being there, and also because he'd still be half-cut. To top that, well, Charlie was such an unknown quantity these days. The unpredictable giant who'd done the most unpredictable thing yet. Just showed up without warning after all this long time. And now what? Keith wasn't sure he knew.

Everything had changed now, since the crash, and he wasn't sure he even knew his oldest brother any more. Yes, he'd always been a bastard to those who had wronged him, but never to the family. *Never*. Family mattered to Charlie. Well, it always seemed to before. When he was home he'd always have a joke and a grin to share. Yes, a bit of ribbing where it was warranted, a bit of ticking off and straightening out if that was needed, and that was fair enough. But, always for Keith at least, a bit of fun, a spot of impromptu shadow boxing.

Not any more, though. Since the crash, it was like the real Charlie had gone and had been replaced with this violent ogre who had a grudge with the world and every one of its inhabitants. And perhaps that included family too these days.

'Why does he get in such a mess, Mam?' Keith asked as Annie handed him his tea. 'I know it was bad, what happened to Betty and the baby and everything, but it's been so long, and it was an accident, after all. Everyone knew that. Could have happened to anyone in that weather. And he had that house and everything. Why did he walk away from all that? My mates say he's kipping on a bench by Rawson Market, and spends all day scrounging money for booze. Is that true? That's a proper showing up, that is, Mam. That's not our Charlie.'

'Keith, shut it!' Annie snapped, surprising him with her sudden vehemence. Pound to a penny that was exactly what had been on her mind too. 'And if you hear any more of your mates talking about him behind his back,' she hissed, 'I expect you to give 'em a bleeding crack, do you hear?' She waggled an admonishing finger at him. 'He's a grown man, you hear? He can do what he frigging well likes!'

Keith would have answered. To his mind, Charlie doing what he liked was the worst thing *for* Charlie. But they both became aware of raised voices in the front room.

Keith put his jar of tea down and turned around to see what was going on. If his dad was up now, he'd be nashing as fast as he could. Charlie and his dad arguing could only lead to one thing these days – bloodshed and drama. And Keith wasn't currently in the mood for either.

But it wasn't his dad, after all. It was Ronnie who'd arrived, and he was now getting it both barrels.

'You're a soft twat!' Charlie was yelling, having got himself half off the sofa. He was still sitting on it with Ronnie in front of him like a naughty school kid standing in front of a head-master. Keith decided Charlie looked even more of a state sitting up. 'No wonder he's taking you for a ride!' he was bark-ing at Ronnie. 'Or to put it correctly, he's taking your *wife* for a ride, while you're a home minding her bleeding kids! What the frigging hell is *wrong* with you?'

Ronnie was looking as sick as a parrot, and hung his head while his older brother carried on ranting at him. *C'mon, Ron*, Keith thought. *At least stand up for yourself!*

'That bleeding wife of yours is a prozzy, Ron,' Charlie thun-dered. 'Always has been, always will be. And that frigging idiot, Butler, is taking the piss!'

Keith thought Charlie was probably right about that. He'd known Jean before Ronnie and he'd heard his mam say more than once that she reckoned Jean had only gone with Ronnie because he thought he had a bit of money, same as Charlie.

And then got pregnant, giving him no choice but to marry her. And then had another one, and all. Ronnie looked defeated, Keith reckoned, and he made his usual mental note; he was never going to let that happen to *him*.

'It might be just rumours, Charlie,' Ronnie finally ventured, even though Keith knew full well it wasn't. 'You know what people are like. Tongues wagging and all that. I mean, I know Jean likes a good time – a drink and that – but, come *on*, I can't see her falling for Tommy Butler.'

Charlie jumped up from the couch and lunged for his brother with surprising agility. He grabbed him by the throat and pushed him up against the front wall. Annie's hand flew to her mouth and Keith held his breath, hoping his dad didn't decide to come down at that moment. As displays of brotherly concern went it didn't feel very helpful.

'Look, you bleeding *idiot*,' Charlie said, 'you know as well as I do what's going on. I'm warning you, Ronnie, you best get it sorted, or *I* will. I'm not having folk thinking that Tommy bleeding Butler is taking the piss out of our family, do you hear?'

Keith sighed. As if that was going to happen. Ronnie wasn't like the rest of them. He'd defend himself if Tommy Butler started but he'd never start anything himself. He didn't like that kind of trouble. Never had.

He nodded anyway, probably because he was currently being half-strangled. Charlie let him loose just as Malcolm walked in. He was rubbing his eyes, having clearly only just woken up, because, as usual, he hadn't gone to school. It wouldn't be long, though – they'd probably hear any day now about another approved school, and that would be the last of him they'd see for a few months. He came, he went. Though nothing ever seemed to change much.

'What's all the noise for?' Malcolm grumbled and then, even as he was thinking better of it, had to dodge a slap round the head. 'Mam,' he yelled immediately, 'our Charlie's starting on me for frig all!'

Keith turned to Annie who was by now standing at the back door having a cigarette. 'You best go in there, Mam,' he whispered, even though Charlie's roars could wake the dead. 'They'll have me dad up in a minute if they're not careful.'

Annie threw her cigarette into the backyard. 'I'm past caring,' she told him. 'They can bleeding kill each other for all I care. Roll on 11 o'clock when the pub opens and I can get out of here for a drink. You lot are driving me mad.'

It didn't look like Joe Laine was calling for Keith that morning, so he resigned himself, at least for the immediate future, to either calling for Titch again or spending some unavoidable time in the company of his family; one who looked and smelled like a tramp, one who was waiting to be sent away – again – and one who was currently bringing shame on the lot of them. He braced himself as he joined them in the front room.

'All right, Ronnie?' he said, feeling sorry for his older brother. 'You come for a sup of tea? Only me mam's got the water on in the back room.'

It seemed to at least break the ice, and though Charlie shook his head at Ronnie he at least seemed to decide he couldn't be bothered shouting any more.

'I'll have a jar, Mam,' he grunted, stomping past Keith, Malcolm and Ronnie, and though the air in the back room soon became as odious as in the front room, they were soon round the table with Annie, eating dripping and bread and companionably drinking tea. Charlie had even taken his jacket off. There were limits, however. Though Annie ventured to suggest there was an old suit upstairs that might be big enough to fit him, the look on Charlie's face made it plain that no one in their right mind would suggest that he might need a bath.

Even so, there seemed an unlikely kind of peace in the room, leading Keith to hope, when his father appeared and walked without speaking to his back-room armchair – as opposed to opting for the one in the front room, further away – that they might even be spared the explosion everyone had been braced for since Charlie had turned up out of the blue.

Annie immediately leapt up from the table and as Reggie scowled at her – his indication that he was expecting bread and tea – rushed to give him his paper to read. No one else spoke, of course – it just wasn't worth it after their dad had had a night on the ale – but as he retreated behind his paper Keith felt the tension lessen slightly. Perhaps he just couldn't be bothered. He hoped so.

But by the time Annie had supplied Reggie with food and drink it was 11 o'clock, and as promised – or, rather, threatened – and much to Reggie's annoyance, she announced that she was off down the pub. A slick of red lipstick and a bit of the same rubbed into her cheeks, she ran a comb through her waves and snatched up her handbag. 'See how you like it, mister,' she threw back at him as her parting shot, 'when *I* come rolling home after a few whiskies.'

Reggie yelled what he always did at the freshly slammed door. 'You're a wicked woman, you are, Annie Hudson!' he barked, before glowering at his sons as if daring them to comment, and taking himself and his paper into the front room.

Charlie and Ronnie, their differences apparently now forgotten, resumed the conversation they'd been having before Annie'd left. They'd been talking boxing – so Charlie was still interested in that, at least, Keith thought – about some big names from down south that were apparently on their way north. 'To take on some of our boys, apparently,' Charlie was telling Ronnie. 'Cockney twats.' He chuckled, and as he did so Keith could see glimpses of the old Charlie. 'Here, Ron,' Charlie went on. 'Now there's a thought. I wonder if it were them that trained our Bob!'

Ronnie laughed too. 'Imagine that! And I'll tell you something else I found out. They're not only after taking our titles. They've got our names an' all. I swear to God, all three of 'em, Charlie. They're brothers too – Charlie's the eldest and Reggie and Ronnie are twins. Kray, they're called. Pretty big-time gangsters too, so I've heard.'

Charlie nodded. 'I've heard that too. Nasty buggers, apparently. Some of lads in Blackpool said they've got business in

Manchester already. Probably won't be long before they move even further north, I suppose.'

Once again, Keith was about to open his mouth and join in when, without warning, Charlie leapt up, knocking over the remains of his tea. He looked pointedly at Ronnie, who suddenly looked as though he was about to shit himself, and then turned and ran through to the front room. Keith and Malcolm followed, exchanging shrugs about what the hell might be going on, but when they heard the familiar clip-clopping sound of a horse and cart coming up the road the penny dropped. Tommy Butler was doing his rounds.

Now there'd be trouble. No doubt about it. 'Coal for hole!' came the chirpy voice from the street. 'Send out your wives and daughters! Send out your grannies if you want!' Reggie had put down his newspaper and removed his broken reading glasses. 'Don't you dare!' he warned, staring at Charlie.

Ronnie paced nervously. 'Charlie, leave it. I swear it, I'll sort him out in the pub next time I see him. Look, I know Jean's doing the dirty, okay? *Okay*? I know she is. I'm just biding my time, that's all. I'll sort it when I'm ready.'

He sounded desperate, but now it looked like there might be a ruckus Keith felt an unexpected excitement in his belly. He watched Charlie very slowly roll up each of his shirt sleeves, while keeping his gaze – and his glare – full on his dad. Keith saw the sinews in his enormous forearms bulge. He might look a state but he obviously wasn't in one – not so you'd notice. Could be an interesting morning after all.

Charlie spoke to Reggie then. 'I'm not asking for your permission, Dad,' he said quietly. 'Keep your nose out. That Tommy Butler is asking for it, and I'm about to give him it. And that's happening whether you like it or not.'

He then turned to Ronnie, who was standing just inside the window with Malcolm. 'You coming outside, or would you rather hide away in here?'

'Don't, Charlie,' Ronnie pleaded. 'He'll think I'm soft if you go out there and he knows I'm in here.'

'You *are* bleeding soft!' Charlie growled as he walked towards the front door. Another door slammed then, and Keith spun his head round to see that his dad had disappeared – he'd obviously taken himself off to the back. The radio started blaring then. He'd obviously ramped up the volume. But, not wanting to miss anything that was about to happen out front, Keith went to join Ronnie and Malcolm at the window. Or, rather, Malcolm – Ronnie was hiding behind the piece of makeshift curtain, and was dependent on his younger brothers to tell him what was going on.

'He's stopped his cart,' Keith informed him, watching it grind to a stop, just outside the Jaggers' house opposite. Harry Jagger, young Annie's boyfriend, had just emerged from his house to watch the unfolding drama as well. Which didn't surprise Keith – this had been inevitable and people had been long expecting it. Just not expecting Charlie to be the one dishing it out. Keith reached up to open the top window so they could hear better.

'Now then, Charlie,' Tommy greeted him, still in the seat of his cart and holding tight to his horse's reins. 'You after a bit o' coal?'

Charlie smiled at him. 'Are you going to get down and have it like a man?' he asked.

Tommy glanced nervously up and down the street. 'Probably wondering if he's got any allies in the vicinity,' Keith explained to Ronnie.

'What's up, Charlie?' Tommy asked, still gripping tightly to his reins. 'Cos if this is about your Ronnie, me and him have already sorted it out.' He glanced towards the house then. 'Go and ask him if you don't believe me.'

There was a moment of silence as the two men stared at each other. But it wasn't a long one. Charlie obviously wasn't in the mood for further chat and his arm shot out as if propelled by some superhuman force, his right hand gripping the coal-man's scrawny neck.

He was up out of the saddle in an instant, reins and all, and was soon dangling, both feet swaying, beside the cart, his heels knocking against it as Charlie held him there. Keith heard Charlie's fist hit his face first and then the unmistakable and sickening sound of his head butt. It was like a whip had cracked. Tommy slumped to the floor as soon as he was released.

'What's happening?' Ronnie wanted to know.

'He's decked him,' Malcolm observed dryly. 'What d'you think?'

Only then did Ronnie dare to come out from behind the curtain. 'Fucking hell fire!' he said. 'He's out for the count!'

The brothers grinned as Harry Jagger caught their eye and stuck his thumbs up from across in his front garden. But it seemed Charlie hadn't finished yet. Stepping purposefully over Tommy Butler's prone form in the middle of the road, he calmly unhitched the seemingly untroubled carthorse from its yoke.

'Oh-uh,' said Malcolm. 'What d'you think he's gonna do now?'

They got their answer a second later. Grabbing the side of the heavily laden cart with both hands, Charlie roared and found the strength to tip it over onto its side, so that the sacks of coal started tipping into the street.

'Coal for fuck all!' he yelled at the top of his voice, to the great delight of all the neighbours who'd clustered to watch the action from their various doorways. They began scurrying out armed with sacks, bowls and buckets, and even suitcases, to collect the black treasure that had now fallen in glistening heaps at their feet.

'We need to get ourselves some o' that!' Malcolm said, dashing out the back to grab an empty sack and join the scrum.

Malcolm was back in a matter of moments, having managed to haul an almost full sack of coal into the house. 'You're good for summat, then!' Keith observed, grinning. They'd have a pretty decent fire in tonight. They soon stopped laughing when their breathless big brother walked back into the house, though, his expression stony and brushing coal dust from his hands.

As if there was any point. They were filthy before he'd started. 'And *you*,' Charlie said, pointing a big finger into Ronnie's face, 'are lucky that you're not getting the same. Don't ever bleeding show me up again, you hear? Now go home and get that mucky bint out of your house, like you should have done months ago, okay?'

Ronnie nodded, but then Charlie's gaze shifted past him, and Keith wondered what had suddenly caught his attention. 'What are you looking at?' Charlie continued, staring over Keith's head.

Keith turned to see his dad in the back-room doorway. He was standing staring at Charlie as though he wanted to kill him.

'Who the bleeding *hell* do you think you are?' Reggie asked, his voice low and angry. 'I want you gone. Gone right now, you hear. You're not welcome here. I don't care what your mother says. Now piss off and keep your trouble away from our bleeding house.'

'He was just standing up for me, Dad,' Ronnie said quietly.

This seemed to inflame their father all the more. 'I've brought up sissies and a fucking animal!' he raged before turning back to Charlie. Keith winced. His dad never used words like that. 'You!' he said, flecks of spittle gathering in the corner of his mouth. 'Look at you. Think you're something special? Leader of the pack, eh? Well, you're not. Never were and never will be, not by a long shot.' He stabbed a finger towards the lino. 'The lad who would have been is six feet under, you hear? You'll *never* be that lad, whatever nonsense your bleeding mother's put between your ears. So go on, piss off out of here, and don't come back.'

Keith stood there stunned, waiting for the next punch to fly. His mam had always said his dad had got it in for Charlie. He didn't understand why – he never had. None of the boys had, not really. It was just a family thing that *was*, like their Eunice being not quite like the others, like him being so scrawny, like Malcolm getting in fights all the time.

Did his dad even mean it? How *could* he mean it? Charlie was his own flesh and blood. They had the same nose. The same hair. The same way of sniffing, their mouths to one side, when they were in the boxing ring and about to throw a killer punch. How could he feel like that? How could he hurt Charlie like that? What had Charlie ever done to deserve it? Except not be Frank. And how could he do anything about that?

'Come on, Dad,' he began, almost automatically. It was like he couldn't help it.

His father glared at him and then he jabbed a finger towards the floor again. '*And* our Brian,' he snarled, still looking daggers at Charlie. 'Did for him as well, didn't you? *Didn't* you? Go on, piss off out of here,' he finished. 'You're dead to me.'

Keith gasped, hearing that, and now the air rushed to escape from him. What would happen now? What would Charlie do next? He looked at his oldest brother, and waited for the inevitable to happen, but to his surprise there was no fist flying towards his dad, no roar of fury, only silence, even though if ever his dad had given him reason to hit him back, it was now.

Yet he didn't. Without taking his eyes off his father, Charlie slowly turned down his shirt sleeves, wiped the blood from his fist across the top of his trousers and then reached for his crumpled jacket, which was on the newel post where he'd draped it. He then turned to nod at Keith, Malcolm and Ronnie in turn, and walked out of the house. Not a word, and not a single glance back.

Reggie sat back down in his chair, picked up his crossword and glasses and returned to his paper. 'You three as well,' he growled. 'You best piss off out of my way an' all.'

Scrabbling to gather trousers and a pullover for Malcolm, the three finally left the house as well. Of Charlie there wasn't a sign, and of the coal there wasn't either. Not so much as a shard of it was left – only dust. Just the sound of the bemused horse quietly snickering beside the upturned cart, and a woman from further up the street helping Tommy Butler to his feet. They had their backs to them, and Keith was glad for Ronnie's sake.

They began to walk down the street, but no one knew what to say. The silence in their brother's wake was just too deafening.

Chapter 18

December 1954

Charlie grunted, semi-conscious, and flicked an arm across his face. It felt raw. And very cold. And something was pricking at his skin too; something cold and unpleasant. He pinched the bridge of his nose, struggling to haul his eyelids open. Then held the back of his hand up to meet his sleepy gaze. Only then did he realise. It was snowflakes. Frigging snowflakes!

He grunted again as he shifted his bulk on the bench. It was the early hours of Monday morning – three or four o'clock, he reckoned. And though the ale he'd drunk had ensured he'd been warm since he'd crashed there, he now realised just how cold it was.

How cold *he* was. 'Bastard snow!' he muttered, as he dragged stiff legs down to the pavement and equally stiff arms and hands onto the freezing bench so he could push himself up into a sitting position. It hadn't been snowing long, but it was now falling thickly. He shook a dusting of the bastard stuff off his head, thighs and arms.

The street was deserted. There was no sign of life bar a distant cat mewling. Given the bitter cold, only a madman would be out on the streets. And why was he? He tried to scroll back to the events of the previous evening, work out what series of altercations might have led him here in this weather. Yes he was mad – mad as hell – but not *that* mad. Much as he preferred the solitude of his bench, he was fairly sure he'd found himself a warm bed – and a warm female body – for the night. The thought made him smile. That would have been rich. Kicked out by one of his own prozzies! And probably the case, he decided, pragmatically.

He scanned the now deserted top end of the town centre before leaning to look underneath the bench to see what might be there. He tended to leave stuff; the odd blanket or pullover, and sometimes food as well. No one would ever dare interfere with it. He was in luck. There was a bottle of someone's home brew and a brown paper bag tucked under the slats, and as he pulled them out he dimly remembered the bag might contain a couple of pork pies from Philip Smiths, the butcher's down Ivegate. He'd often help him out with the odd pie or pasty if Charlie was passing by, so these days Charlie made a point of passing by all the time.

He placed the bottle between his feet for a moment and unrolled the bag. It was indeed pork pies, a brace of them, the sight alone enough to make his stomach clench. He tried to work out when he'd last eaten. But that was the trouble with being sober; it always made him think. And doing too much of that was never helpful. So he stopped himself and plunged his teeth into the pie-crust instead, concentrating hard on the oily coldness that spread in his mouth, chewing mechanically, watching the flakes twirling downwards and settling around him.

But it was no good. The thoughts came anyway. And thinking made him angry. The bastard cold made him angry. The bastard snow made him angry. Snow was Christmas. And Christmas always reminded him of parties, which reminded him of the thing he never wanted to think about again.

'Bastard December!' he shouted up into the dark skies, feeling between his legs for the bottle that would make the thoughts go away. But it was frozen. He couldn't even get the bulging cork from the top. He hurled it across the path and onto the triangle of grass opposite. 'Bastard December!' he yelled again into the silence. 'Come on, yer bastards! Come on!'

He didn't even know what or whom he was shouting to. He just knew he needed someone to come and tell him to shut up. It would be hours yet before the bastard pubs opened.

No one did. If the nearby pub landlords could hear him, none put their lights on. And if any passing policemen in their right minds had heard him, he knew they would have made a detour to avoid him. Charlie was alone and there was nothing else to do but get back on his bench and wait for opening time.

Somehow, life had developed a kind of pattern. And in an ironic, and what felt like the most inappropriate, kind of twist, the new Charlie that had been created from the ashes of his old life had become more respected and notorious than ever. Did folk pity him? He wasn't sure and he had no way of knowing, since he kept every shred of emotion he felt at arm's length, and people knew to broach the subject of the crash at their peril. But there was certainly a look that would come over certain people's faces – especially women – that he knew held compassion for what had happened to him.

Except it hadn't happened to him. He had been the one to make it happen. And to his mind, right-thinking people should have hated him for it. Not that it mattered much either way, really. There wasn't a person walking the earth who could hate him as much as he hated himself.

And business, as a consequence, was booming. He could work twice as many hours as he had any sort of mind to as there wasn't a loan shark or scrap or used car dealer who didn't want him to be their minder. These days he was the best kind of hired muscle around – one without fear or forbearance – enabling those who employed him to continue doing what they did best: ripping people off.

He was also earning well from his gambling dens and whore-houses, even if his input in the running of them was minimal. And there was a fight for him any time or anywhere he wanted one, and, without ties – or any concern about what might happen in his absence – he'd head off and get in the ring anywhere the fancy took him, from the south coast to the east and even to Ireland.

He'd still yet to lose a fight and he wasn't just a brawler, either; he had the skills he needed to make a fine professional boxer. There was still the odd trainer trying hard to get him to quit the drink and do it, too, but whatever thoughts he'd once had about making the leap had long since gone down the drain, washed away by the torrential rain that late December night.

Charlie had always had his own ideas about the Queensberry Rules anyway, but now he'd think nothing of half-strangling or head-butting an opponent if they really riled him and, once in the ring now, he got riled rather a lot. He had little appetite any more for the kind of professionalism required, either. His appetite these days was for oblivion more than anything. Something only women and drink could provide.

He was standing at the Unicorn bar now, having just seen off the last of his women, and draining the last dregs of a gill of ale. He'd been in since opening time, as he usually was when he didn't have anything else doing, keeping an eye on his girls, and the kind of punters they were hooking up with – important for the latter to be in no doubt, from time to time, who they'd be dealing with if they tried to rip them off.

But with the last of them now finally hooked up with a client, he was done for the day. Well, in terms of work, at least. He wasn't done with drinking – not by a long shot. Though Ray the landlord definitely was; it was four o'clock now, and the pub had all but emptied.

'Gi's another one in this, Ray,' he said, passing his glass over.

Ray had been watching the clock for a good half hour now, Charlie knew. 'One more then,' he said, pulling the beer, 'but I'm shutting up shop for an hour or two at half past.' He placed the glass on the empty bar. 'There you go,' he said. 'On the house, lad.'

Charlie chuckled. He'd been drinking 'on the house' all day long, so it wasn't likely he'd be paying for this one. Not that he felt sorry for Ray, not really. He wasn't daft when it came to his beer. He knew plenty of people would have already paid for drinks for him; they'd have left them 'in' behind the bar. It made life less complicated, Charlie mused as he picked up the glass. Being paid in kind made more sense than being paid in hard cash – it would be going on beer mostly, anyway, so it sort of cut out the middle man.

'Cheers, pal,' he said, raising the glass and taking a swig. 'And I'll be off after this one, so don't start crapping yourself.'

Ray nodded hopefully and went off to start clearing the remaining tables, but he'd barely started when the door opened and, along with a blast of cold and snow, admitted a big man in a heavy black overcoat.

'Chuck Hudson!' he boomed, and Charlie chuckled again as Ray's shoulders slumped in resignation. He raised a hand in greeting and the man crossed the bar in a couple of strides. 'I've been looking all over the bleeding town for you, old pal,' he said, extending a hand for Charlie to shake. 'Good to find you at last. How are you doing?'

The man was Darley Adams, a local fighter and trainer. One of the men who'd spent a lot of time trying to urge Charlie to go professional back in the day. Back at a time when keeping fit and boxing were both priorities for Charlie. Back before *then*.

He'd not seen Darley in ages and, in as much as he could feel pleasure in anything currently, he was pleased to see his old sparring partner now. Though he had no idea why he'd been so keen to track him down. 'Now then, Darley!' he said, clapping his old friend on the back delightedly. It wasn't just the beer. His day had just got one hundred per cent better. 'What brings you back to shitty Bradford?' he asked, yanking out one of Ray's already tidied-away bar stools. 'I thought you were living the bleeding high life in Blackpool. The "King of Winter Gardens", isn't it? That's what I've heard.'

Darley laughed and, ignoring the stool for a moment, took a long slow look at Charlie. 'Bloody hell,' he said finally. 'What's with the get-up? You fallen on hard times, mate, or what?'

Charlie's expression hardened. Where to start? Instead, he looked around for the landlord and shouted across to him. 'Ray! We need two more over here.' Then, seeing Ray's expression, added, 'Don't worry, we'll be off after this. I just need to have a few words with my old pal here.'

Ray duly supplied the drinks and went to sit in a booth by the window, a look of resignation on his face. He knew as well as Charlie did that the pub would close when they'd finished and no sooner.

'So,' Charlie said, tilting his fresh glass towards Darley, 'like I said before, what brings you here?'

'You, Charlie boy,' Darley replied, pulling the bar stool beneath him. 'Got a bit of business for you if you want it. Very good money.'

'What sort of business?' Charlie asked.

'*Good* business,' Darley told him 'And probably right up your street. And,' he added, raising a finger and jabbing it towards Charlie's chest, 'they even asked for you personally.'

'They being?'

'The Krays,' he said. 'You know the oldest one already, don't you?'

'Charlie? Yes. I've run into him a couple of times. Did a bit of minding for him down in Kent a couple of months ago, and we were in the nick for a few weeks together a while back.'

'And he's not forgotten you, by all accounts,' Darley went on. 'He obviously knows you can handle yourself – your reputation precedes you. Only one thing, though – there's a condition attached. They need you to be sober.'

'I can be sober if I need to be,' Charlie said. 'If I feel it's worth it, at any rate. So what *is* the job?' Probably a fight someone had set up, he guessed. He hadn't fought for money for over a year – these days he earned a living mostly from knocking the fight out of other people – but he was suddenly interested. Maybe that was what he needed. Maybe a few bouts in the ring would do him good.

'It's not a fight, Charlie,' Darley said, obviously guessing his train of thought. 'It's a spot of minding, but, like I said, it pays very well. More than me and you are used to getting from a fight, as it happens.'

'Minding,' Charlie repeated, slightly disappointed. Was that all? He could get plenty of minding work on his own right here in Bradford. Yes, minding wasn't a bad earner, and it would give him the excuse he needed to land a few crippling blows now and again. But minding was just minding. It would have to be made worth his while. 'So who needs minding? What is it, bookies, scrappers, what?'

'Neither,' Darley said. 'You know his younger brothers, yes? Ronnie and Reggie?'

Charlie nodded. Where exactly was this going? They were supposed to be bleeding hard men, those Kray twins. 'Why the frigging hell would they need a minder?' he asked Darley.

'I can't name names, Charlie, as you know, but they need a team of four from up north. There's me, you and two Blackpool wrestlers involved if you're in. We have to reckon to be minders for the Kray brothers and their associates.'

'Reckon?' Charlie said. 'Darley, talk sense. Will we be minding them or not?'

Darley glanced around the pub and moved his stool closer to Charlie. 'Thing is, pal,' he said, lowering his voice, even though there was only Ray there to hear them. 'I'm sure you know what they're into at the moment: drugs and guns. Well, it seems they've stepped out of their territory and upset a few of the big boys in Manchester. In particular one mean bastard known as Glasgow Henry. Anyway, Charlie Kray has a fight on at the Winter Gardens and the twins are seeing it as an opportunity to show their defiance.' He lowered his voice further. 'Against the northerners who've told them not to cross the Watford Gap.'

Charlie nodded. 'But that hasn't answered my question, Darley. What do you mean by we have to "reckon" to be minders?'

'Well, see, the boys don't have minders. It's like you just said. It's bad form to look like you can't fight your own battles. So what they're after is something a bit more discreet. What they want is for us to don smart suits, which they'll pay for,' he added, nodding towards Charlie's crumpled attire, 'and just to mingle in with their "associates". If there's trouble from a rival gang, we're part of the Krays' team, simple as that. They don't want it known that they're paying for a few hard nuts, obviously. Just want it to seem like we're "all mates together", kind of thing.'

Charlie laughed, causing Ray, who'd nodded off by the window, to jump. '"Associates"! You even sound like one of the Cockney twats, Darley! Though "associate" will do me well enough if the money's right. How much?'

'Like I said, Charlie, I have to assure them that you'll be sober. That you'll actually turn up, an' all. Once that's set in stone, it's …' Darley leaned in till his mouth was by Charlie's ear. 'Forty pounds apiece, Charlie. Forty pounds, plus a weekend in the best digs in Blackpool and a made-to-measure suit to boot. What do you say?'

Forty pounds was a small fortune. And for a weekend's work that might even include a belter of a fight, only a fool would knock it back. 'I'm in,' Charlie said, grinning.

Darley held out his hand to shake Charlie's. 'And can I count on you, mate, to be …'

'Sober? Oh yes,' Charlie said. 'For forty smackers I'll be sober. I might even head to the public baths and have a proper wash.'

Chapter 19

Keith rolled his eyes as he walked in the house. It was the week before Christmas, and as usual there was a houseful. He'd just finished work – painting the inside of a semi on the next street – and was hoping to be greeted by the meaty onion smell of a stew bubbling away on the range.

No such luck. It was his ears that were assaulted, rather than his nose, by the sound of squawking kids and raucous laughter. Raucous *adult* laughter, mostly, even though it was only just half five. *Great*, he thought, kicking the snow from his boots in the hallway. Were his mam and dad on the ale already?

He walked into the front room. Annie and Reggie were obviously in good spirits, anyway. June was round with little Lyndsey, and her brand new baby, Vinnie, who she was cradling while she stood and warmed her backside. That there was a fire crackling in the first place was a good sign, as well. It meant they had money for once.

And had obviously drunk some of it, too, judging by his mam's silly giggle, as she poured gloopy yellow liquid from a jug into a jar for him. 'Here, our Keith,' she said, 'have a cup of egg-nog to warm you up.' She handed the jar to him, which smelled pretty pungent. He downed it anyway. Might as well as not.

'Cheers, Mam,' he said, 'it has. But is there owt on for tea?' He glanced through to the back room, where Ronnie, young Joe and David were sitting at the table. They seemed to be eating already.

'My Jock had a win on the horses,' June said, 'so he's brought a barrow load of chips round. Go on, Keith,' she said, motioning for him to go and dig in. 'Help yourself, our kid, before them greedy gets eat them all.'

Keith didn't need telling twice. He was soon seated at the big table, and as always the younger ones stopped picking up chips until Keith had loaded a square of torn-up newspaper with as many as he wanted. Now he was a grown-up, he was pleased about the rule he'd grown up hating. As a worker himself, he could at last see the logic in his mam insisting that the workers take precedence.

But there were plenty of chips piled up in the centre of the table, loaded with salt and steaming with vinegar. Keith was partial to his stews and dumplings, but chips were filling enough. At 17 he was practically a man, and with a day of hard grafting under his belt he had an appetite like a man as well.

'What's new, then?' he asked his brothers as they could at last get stuck in. Not that he needed to ask when it came to Ronnie, who looked just the same as he did every day – bloody miserable. After the incident with Tommy Butler, Jean had left him and her two boys that very day. They'd moved somewhere miles away from Bradford, apparently, and said she didn't care what happened to the kids; they'd been shipped off to an orphanage that same week.

Since then, it was as if his marriage had never even happened. He was now either back round his mam's morning noon and night or, more often than not, out on the beer.

'Our Malcolm might be home for Christmas,' Joe ventured. Then he frowned. 'And me dad's drunk. He just kissed me mam in front of everybody.'

David and Joe started giggling as they watched Keith's face contort in horror. 'Bleeding hell, he *must* be pissed!' he said.

He glanced into the front room where he could see him telling Jock some tale or other. Jock had married their June when she fell pregnant with her first – little Lyndsey who was now around two, if Keith remembered rightly. He seemed a decent enough bloke and was mates with Annie's chap, Harry Jagger.

Much as it pleased Keith to see his dad in a good mood for a change, he knew better than to think it might last. He turned back to his chips, hoping it would at least last a little bit longer. He was tired and in no mood for shouting tonight.

Or sitting with folk who had faces like wet weekends, for that matter. 'What's up with you, Ronnie? You look like you've lost a shilling and found a penny.'

'Nowt,' Ronnie said, maungy and miserable as ever. 'Just got a headache, that's all. Go get me some of that egg-nog will you? I could do with a drink.'

That was rich, thought Keith, after he'd been working all day while his brother had been on the ale. He'd half a mind to tell him to piss off, but he didn't because the rules were still the rules. The younger one did what the older one ordered.

'Here, Keith,' June called as he went to get it. She had a cigarette hanging from her teeth and held out the most recent addition to the family. June had had him just two weeks ago, and he was a right bleeding screamer. 'Hold Vincent a minute for me, will you, while I go and have my ciggie.'

Keith shook his head. 'I'm not holding him,' he said. 'I'm all acky. Give him to Jock or me dad to hold. I need a wash and that first.'

Keith grabbed some of the egg-nog for Ronnie and made a swift exit back to the table.

'Have you heard owt about our Charlie?' he asked, passing Ronnie the drink.

'Not since he got back from Blackpool,' Ronnie answered, sitting back in his seat. 'People are saying he was involved with some Irish gang from Manchester, though. Summat to do with them Kray lads. I don't know if it's true, but apparently there was guns, machetes and razors involved, and some bloke from Glasgow had his hand severed.'

Keith shook his head. 'Our Charlie doesn't fight with weapons, Ronnie. Never has and never would. Why the frig would he need a weapon with fists like he's got?'

Ronnie pulled a face. 'I'm just saying what I've heard, that's all. They reckon the police are on to it too. That's probably why no one's seen hide nor hair of our Charlie.'

'Will he go to the bad boys' place like our Malcolm?' young David asked. At eight now, he was already getting wise to the ways of the family. Ronnie reached out and swotted him round the head.

'Bedtime for you, lad. What've I told you about kids, eh?'

'Should be seen and not heard,' David whispered, rubbing his head. He slid from his chair and reached for Joe. 'You coming up, our Joe?'

'I'm bloody 11, David,' Joe snapped, looking appalled at the very suggestion. 'Three years older than *you*. So, no, I'm not frigging coming yet!'

'Oh yes you are,' Ronnie said, reaching across to give him a slap too.

Keith laughed as he watched his young brothers scarper. 'They know far too bleeding much for their age, that little pair of swines. Anyway, like I was saying, Ronnie, I wouldn't pay too much attention to all that crap about Charlie. He's not daft enough to get involved with that stuff. And I'm telling you, he wouldn't use weapons.' He balled the paper his chips had been in and wiped his mouth on the back of his arm. 'C'mon, let's get ourselves a bit of that fire, shall we?'

It was almost too hot in the front room with everyone in it, Annie rocking the baby in her arms now, as June was smoking yet again, and Reggie and Jock still sat gabbing about Jock's dad and the antics he used to get up to in the Punch Bowl.

'C'mon, Keith,' June said, laughing, 'who d'you think he most looks like? Me or Jock?'

'Don't laugh, Keith,' Annie said. 'You know, what with his hair being red, an' all. But you know who he *most* reminds me of? Our Charlie. You know, when he was a baby. He's the spit.'

Suddenly, the atmosphere changed completely. Even though Keith didn't think he'd even been listening to their conversation, Reggie Snr slammed his jar down on the floor and immediately stood up. 'How many times, eh?' he said, staggering over to Annie and stabbing at her chest with his finger. 'How many times have I told you not to mention that waste of bleeding space in my house?'

'Shut your bleeding face, Reggie Hudson,' she shot back. 'I'll mention my son whenever I bleeding like. How many times have I told *you* that?'

June reached in between them and retrieved baby Vincent. 'Aw, Mam, Dad, knock it off. We're having a good night. Don't spoil it.'

Reggie turned then. 'You shut your cake hole, June. This is *my* house. My business.'

Ronnie nudged Keith. 'I'm off. I'll come back when they're all in bed. I'm not staying here to listen to this crap.'

Keith had been thinking exactly the same. He glanced at little Lyndsey, who was curled up, fast asleep on the sofa, her curls falling in golden curls across her face. She looked like an angel, and he wondered how long it would be before the crap

Ronnie'd alluded to all became normal for her – people shouting and scrapping and drinking, day in day out. It was a miracle she hadn't woken up as it was. She would do soon, though, and when he caught Jock's eye he could see he was thinking the same thing himself. 'I think I'd better get our June and the kids home,' he whispered. He shook his head, as Annie and Reggie started arguing in earnest. 'Looks like this could get nasty.'

Keith agreed. No matter how well Jock thought he'd been getting along with Reggie, he knew that his dad could turn on his brother-in-law in a heartbeat. If he'd even remembered he was there, which was now debatable. Annie and Reggie were at it hammer and tongs now, yelling drunkenly at each other about what a terrible parent the other was, and how they should burn in hell for it. It never changed. Probably never would. They were like a pair of broken records.

With Jock and June beating a hasty retreat, before the babies started howling, Keith was stuck with the decision about what to do himself. He could bugger off, but to where exactly? And it was a freezing, snowy night out there as well. No, he'd wait it out. He was knackered and wanted to curl up on the sofa – seemed criminal not to, not when there was a fire in. And it was a far better option than getting an early night in and risking getting pissed on by young David; he was eight going on about three where bed-wetting was concerned. No, one of them would give up soon enough and storm off to bed in a temper. He crossed his fingers and sent a silent prayer to God that it was his dad.

His patience paid off. He'd only been sitting on the sofa, reading what was left of the morning paper for a scant 15 minutes, when Reggie, red-faced and spitting feathers, barged past him, screaming at Annie as he left.

'He's a bleeding cuckoo in the nest, Annie Hudson!' he yelled at her. 'You've only got to look at him! He's nothing like me! And he's nothing like his brothers, neither. You're a bleeding muck hook, woman! That's what *you* are!'

'How *dare* you!' Annie shot back, still wielding the empty egg-nog bottle. Go on – piss off, you bleeding madman!' She waggled a finger at him. 'You want to know the truth, do you? I'll tell you the truth, shall I? You hate him because he's *exactly* like you, Reggie Hudson. Just like you but a lot bleeding bigger! Now go to bed and take your filthy mind with you!'

Reggie thundered up the stairs then and Keith put down the paper, while Annie rattled off into the back room, probably after a smoke. He sat and pondered what his dad had said. He knew exactly what a cuckoo in the nest was – some other man's kid. There were lots of kids he knew who had been called that after their dads had come back from the war years ago, but he'd never heard it about any of his brothers or sisters. Their Charlie? What the hell was his dad talking about? They even looked alike. But he knew he'd get a crack if he asked his mam outright, so he left her to it for a few minutes before following her into the back and seeing if she was okay.

Bloody booze, he thought, as she rattled around clearing the table, obviously crying. That was nothing new, not if they'd been drinking half the day, which it seemed like they had. But it was different. This wasn't her furious banging-around kind of crying. She was crying softly, as though she was really upset. He watched her for a moment – there wasn't much to tidy really, just the remaining chip wrappers – and when she went back to sit by the fire he followed her in and sat down next to her on the sofa.

'What's he on about, Mam?' he ventured, righting the jar Reggie had knocked over earlier.

Annie pulled up a corner of her pinny and wiped her face with it. 'Take no notice,' she said. 'He doesn't mean it, Keith. It's just the drink.'

'No it's not, Mam,' he said. 'He's said it before. Not what he just said to you, but the same sort of thing. Is that why he's got it in for our Charlie? Does he *really* think he's another man's kid?'

Annie opened her mouth, and sort of tutted, like she was about to tell him he'd got it wrong. But then she stopped and sighed. 'Who knows what he thinks?' She'd started crying again. 'And who bleeding cares anyway! He's a bastard, your dad. A bad, nasty bastard. Always was, always will be. Whatever he says, he knows full well our Charlie's his. Just didn't want him to be his, that's all.'

Keith tried to understand how his dad could reject his own baby son, especially when he'd lost one already. 'But what did Charlie do to make him hate him?'

'Nothing, Keith,' Annie said softly. 'He was just a baby, wasn't he?' She dabbed at her eyes again, then smoothed her pinny back down. She turned to him then. 'But not Frank. Thing is, Keith,' she said, 'that your dad loved little Frank like you'd not believe, honest you wouldn't. Apple of his eye, he was. Couldn't have been a prouder dad. Taking him everywhere, showing him off to anyone who'd stop and coo at him … And Frank loved him too. When our Margaret came along and I was busy nursing her and so on, he was *always* with his dad. He'd cry every time he walked out of the room, toddle after him with his arms out … And then we lost him. Our first baby boy, Keith, can you imagine? Such a happy little lad he was an' all …'

Her voice trailed off and Keith stroked her arm as he waited for her to continue. He was hearing things he'd never heard before, and he was rapt. 'But I still don't understand. Why's that make my dad hate Charlie?' he pressed. 'That's what I don't understand.'

Annie sighed heavily. 'Son, I wish I knew the answer to that. I really do.' She wiped her face again and stared into the middle distance for a bit. 'Maybe it was partly my fault,' she said eventually. 'He never took to him. Not really, not like he'd taken to Frank. No reason I can think of. He just – well, he just wanted Frank back. And, well, you'll know when you have nippers of your own, things can be hard. We had our Margaret, and she was always a handful, and your dad would come in from work, and, well, he just never seemed to have any time for little Charlie. I don't think he'd got over Frank, that's the truth of it. He didn't *want* Charlie. He wanted Frank back, like I say. On and on all the time about how no one would ever be able to fill his shoes. And maybe that was the problem. But what else was I supposed to do? If he wasn't going to love him, I had to love him even more. The more your dad hated him, the more time I gave him, and that seemed to make him ignore him all the more. Except when he was boxing,' she conceded, sniffing. 'That was the only time he had any time for him. It's no wonder your brother got so good at it, eh? He was so desperate for his dad to be proud of him. But it was always as if he saw him as mine. But he was *our* son, and it wasn't his fault little Frank died, was it?'

Keith tried to process what his mam was telling him. To understand. And perhaps he could. He could see how she must feel, and, perhaps for the first time, he could understand how his dad might have felt too. He stared into the fire, which was beginning to die down and would need some stoking. Either way, there was nothing to be done about it now. Still, now he understood better, perhaps one day he could sit down with Charlie and try to explain it to him.

If that day ever came along now, that was.

Chapter 20

February 1955

Charlie leapt up from the mattress on the floor that he'd been sleeping on. He knew he'd been woken by a noise of some sort, but now there was silence, and he couldn't work out what it had been.

He glanced around the room, which was dimly lit by the glow of an outside street lamp, the feeble light making shadows that shifted across a sea of old fish and chip wrappers, bottles and jars. His eyes strained to see. Was there anything that looked different? It didn't seem so. Gill Anderson, a pisshead he'd recently got to know from Buttershaw, was still sprawled out on the mattress he'd fallen asleep on, along with the haggard prostitute he'd brought home with him the night before.

Edna Berry, the town's mouthiest drunk, was still out for the count too, lying in a pool of her own filth on top of the torn cardboard boxes that were her own makeshift bed. The stench was putrid, even to Charlie's long-habituated nostrils – a blend of stale alcohol, tobacco, farts and filth.

He stepped off the mattress and, taking as much care as he could about what he trod on, crossed the room to the front door, all his senses now on full alert. He didn't know who or what he expected to find. Only that the hairs were standing up on his neck, and it wasn't anything to do with the cold.

The breath was clouding in front of his face even so. It was the beginning of February, and this place had been home for him for a month now, since the particularly bitter winter weather had really set in. It had been the worst in a while and, much as he hated to have to use it, he'd been driven here from his bench out of necessity. A filthy squat owned by the council that had been empty for months, it had become a much-needed winter shelter for the city's vagrants and drunks – not to mention the odd errant husband.

No more, though – not unless Charlie said so, anyway. Since being forced to use it, he'd soon seen off the previous inhabitants, and only when he was feeling particularly generous would he allow anyone else in to join him. And only then if they came bearing gifts.

The squat was situated next door to the Harp of Erin pub on Chain Street, which was its only redeeming feature. That and the fact that it kept him out of sight: he knew full well that people were looking for him. It was this knowledge that kept Charlie on high alert now, and meant he'd only slept lightly, despite the booze. Not that he was afraid. Quite the opposite. He'd had plenty of time to reflect and was quite looking forward to what he knew was likely to be coming: a retaliation attack from at least three men.

And, tucked away up here, he was ready for them. As much as he hated being indoors – particularly with other people – the squat had given him a vital vantage point. The bench was too exposed if the men were to sneak up on him, and this flat had a balcony outside the front door. He could see what was coming if he kept his wits about him, and if he was confronted at the door, well, that would be fine; the balcony would be the last thing his attackers would see as they went sailing overboard.

*   *   *

It had been a bloodbath in Blackpool. A completely different league. He'd met up with Charlie Kray and had gone up there expecting nothing more than a bit of light entertainment; a bit of fighting, a lot of drinking and that promised 40 quid. But what he'd found himself in the middle of had been something rather different – a bloodbath of a kind that really wasn't his style at all, a full-on battle between the Londoners and the Mancs. A messy battle; a number of stabbings, a number of shootings – one lad had had his knee-caps shot to splinters – and some bloody violence that went beyond the sort of thing he usually meted out. One man had had his hand chopped clean off.

Not that Charlie was slow in coming forward and getting involved. Yes, the Krays had done what the Krays were becoming notorious for doing – and he'd never wanted any of that – but Charlie also knew the man he'd taken out personally was still in a coma in Manchester Royal Infirmary.

He had Darley to thank for the information. Intent on retaliation against the Krays, they'd obviously done their homework and stopped off on the way down south to take care of the Bradford contingent they'd roped in. They'd come for him and stabbed him and given him a proper pasting but he'd recovered sufficiently to get the word to Charlie that, sooner or later, they'd be coming for him as well. Might have already done so, by the sound of it, Charlie reckoned, even though he couldn't work out how the hell they'd tracked them down. He moved even more carefully as he approached the door and curled his fingers round his weapon. Assuming the police hadn't got to him first.

It was a possibility it was the coppers out there, but there was no way of knowing. So it was really a case of suck it and see. 'Who's there?' he growled, one hand on the front door latch, the other holding a wooden chair leg in position above his head. There was no answer, but Charlie knew there were people outside. He could hear low whispering on the other side of the thin door.

Nothing for it, then. 'I hope you've said your bleeding prayers,' he added, smiling round bared teeth as he yanked open the door.

Darley had been right. There were three of them, probably the same ones who'd put him in hospital. Three big geezers, all of them suited and booted, two clubs, a blade and a lot of attitude between them.

'Come on, then!' he raged at them. 'Let's fucking have it!' He then swung his lump of wood, as hard and fast as he could, around the biggest of the three's head. He went down like a sack of shit, just as Charlie had expected, but the other two were on him before he'd had a chance to do anything else. He felt the blade being stabbed into his side, his senses now in overdrive, but luckily – courtesy of a range of friendly bypassers and well-wishers – he was insulated by a flannel shirt, three pullovers and a pretty hefty overcoat, so he knew he wouldn't be too badly damaged. He barely felt the punches raining into his head either, nor the club that was being bashed repeatedly into his legs, obviously intended to bring him down.

He had this inability to really feel physical pain these days. Not compared to the other kind. On the contrary. It was almost like a kind of release.

'Fuck off!' he sneered now at the Manc with the blade. 'You're gonna have to do better than that, old pal.' Throwing the chair leg over the balcony, and ignoring the man who'd manoeuvred behind him with the club, Charlie then made a grab for the one in front, grabbing the knife-wielding hand before the man had a chance to slash at him, then slamming it hard and fast against the balcony rail.

It wouldn't need much then, but he was a pro, so he thought he'd give it all he had anyway, and swung an uppercut that he hoped would have made Sugar Ray Robinson wince. He heard the crack of the jaw breaking and capitalised upon it by following up with a right hook to the side of his head.

With number two slumped to the floor, blood beginning to squirt from various orifices, Charlie knew number three wouldn't put up much of a fight. In fact, as he turned, the man was already backing into the flat, palms held high in front of him, in surrender.

It had almost been too easy. 'Ah,' he said, following him in, and gesturing back as he did so. 'Look at your pals, all snuggled up on the landing. Fancy a threesome?'

'Charlie, please,' the man pleaded, looking like he was going to throw up. 'I never even wanted to come. Honest, mate. Not right, this.'

'What do you mean, "not right, this"?' Charlie growled at him, all thoughts of hammering a fist into his weaselly face forgotten. There was something about his expression; the way he'd suddenly caved.

'Giving you up,' the man said, spitting a string of bloody mucus onto the lino. 'Fuckin' southerners. You want to think a bit more carefully about who you work for, in my book.'

The man stood tensed, then, as if waiting for the blows to start coming, now he'd left the script and said his piece. Charlie studied him as he got his breath back and tried to take in what he'd just told him. He was a heavy-set type, in his forties, or thereabouts, with neatly dressed hair, which was greying at the sides. His clothes looked expensively tailored – a good bit pricier than Darley's and his own hastily sewn suits, for sure

– and even in the gloom you could probably see your face in his highly polished shoes. He almost looked like a spiv. But spiv he most definitely wasn't.

Hearing a throat being cleared, Charlie looked beyond him, belatedly realising that his trio of temporary flatmates were all huddled together in the corner, against the back wall. They looked terrified. And they didn't need to be a part of any of this.

Glowering at the Manc, he turned his attention to them. 'You lot, get out!' he said, cocking a thumb back towards the door. 'Go on, piss off, the lot of you. And if I hear a bleeding word said about this, you know what will happen.'

Gill and his recent purchase staggered to their feet and then helped Edna to hers. 'I swear, Charlie,' Gill rasped as they squeezed by him, taking their fetid stench with them, 'not a word about it, lad, not a word.'

There was a clatter in the stairwell as they made their way back down and out into the freezing night. Well, what was left of it, anyway. He reckoned it must be about three in the morning by now. He needed to get his head cleared and decide what best to do.

He turned his attention back to the man he'd been about to beat up and could now see no reason to. Not that he'd taken his eyes off him at any point.

'So, tell me,' he said instead. 'We're the patsies, are we? Your twat of a boss has done a deal with the Krays, has he? Then you and your boys have been suckered in as well, by the looks of it. Make no mistake, if I'd have wanted you crippled or dead I'd have done it, and you Mancs and the Cockneys both know it.'

The man's flash of irritation at this confirmed it. Bleeding prat. Perhaps he'd bust his nose anyway, just to mess up his fancy togs. 'So what's the score?' Charlie asked him. 'Have them London lads got some sort of death wish?'

The man spread his arms. 'Just do what you gotta do,' he said, looking resigned to his fate. 'I can't help you with the politics, mate. All I know is my bosses have got some deal going with the Krays. We were told to sort out loose ends, that's all.' He shrugged apologetically. 'And that's you.'

Charlie took this in, cradling one heavy fist in the other. That jaw had bruised him. But not half as much as what he'd just heard had. The back-stabbing, snivelling bastards. The Mancs hadn't tracked them down – they hadn't had to. The fucking Krays had offered him and Darley up.

He glared at the so-called gangster in front of him. 'You know what?' he said mildly. 'I've half a mind to send you back without a bastard tongue in your head, old pal.'

He let that thought sink in while he thought for a moment longer, pacing back and forth. If the Krays had cut a deal with the Mancs, and the cost had been him and Darley, then there was no reason for this to go any further. Not if they returned to Manchester having squared the account. And knowing how these things worked, there was no chance this two-bit little trio would return and tell 'em the God's honest truth. No, he could keep his nose *and* his tongue; he was going to need it. He had a story to tell.

'I tell you what,' he said, decided. 'Sort your bleeding sissy mates out and then fuck off back to where you came from. If I get so much of a sniff of you in this town tomorrow, you won't be so lucky.'

He stepped onto the landing then, and gave a swift kick in the guts to both of the prone and groaning men. Then he stepped across them. 'Oh, and if you've got any sense,' he said to the man still in the flat, who looked to be in shock at his unexpected luck, 'you'll torch this place as well, before you go.'

He walked along the landing, not even wondering who the neighbours might be, and headed down the fire escape without looking back.

Charlie's bench was empty, with a light patina of frost on it. He sat down heavily, conscious of a slight stinging in his side. He'd been nicked with the blade here and there and he knew he'd feel stiff tomorrow, but right now all his focus was on the exchange that had just taken place. He sat, forearms on knees, in the dead calm of the night, untroubled at the thought of what might happen next. There would be no police on the hunt for him. He knew that now. No, the Cockneys and the Mancs were holding hands together, clearly. Given what had just happened, he knew the whole carry-on would have been covered up. So at least he and Darley didn't have to worry about that.

Whether or not they'd send over more of their cronies was another thing. With any luck, these three would go back and lie. It was the easiest path, after all – to go back and say they'd done what they'd been told to. If they knew what was good for them they would anyway.

He was so lost in thought that it was only a light at the perimeter of his vision that alerted Charlie to the flames that were now licking upwards from the windows of the flat. Good, he thought. So far, they'd done what he'd told them to. Feeling overcome with exhaustion then, he pulled the overcoat tight around him and lay down, half anticipating the sound of the fire engines some good citizen would doubtless have called, but with his mind drifting ever inwards. Fucking twats.

Still, hopefully he'd at least be able to catch a few hours' kip before the morning workers woke him up with their inane jabbering.

Chapter 21

'Charlie, wake up!'

The voice kept saying the same thing, over and over, insistent and hectoring and much too loud in Charlie's ear.

'What the …'

'Charlie, *wake up!*' The same voice. 'You're under arrest for arson. And a possible assault too. On your feet.'

It was Peek. Bleeding Peek. Looking all of 20 going on 12.

The snow had finally stopped falling. All he could hear was the sounds of the morning. People hurrying by. Boots hitting slush. Trams trundling past.

'What the fucking hell are you talking about?' he spluttered, trying to rouse himself. Arson? Assault? What was the idiot on about?

He pulled himself to a sitting position, shaking his head to help the mists clear inside his head. He was so cold he couldn't even bend his fingers. 'You want your head testing, Peek,' he said, rubbing furiously at his eyes. He opened them to see another copper standing beside his nemesis. Looking like the proverbial cat who'd got the bloody cream.

'Come on, Charlie,' said the other copper, shoving an obliging arm under his armpit and yanking hard on it, to try to help him to his feet. 'That's the way,' he said. 'Come along, mate. We don't want no trouble.'

Which was all the more reason to give him some, Charlie thought. He'd not even had his breakfast. And his side hurt.

'Take your bleeding hands off me!' he growled as he rose from the bench.

Peek immediately placed a hand on his over-enthusiastic colleague's arm. 'It's all right, Sam, there'll be no trouble. There's no need to assist our Charlie.'

He glanced at Charlie then, trying to meet his gaze and finally making a connection. 'You'll be all right coming along to the station with us, won't you, pal? Just need to answer a few questions for the time being. That's all. No fuss.'

'What questions?' Charlie asked him, rising to his full height and dwarfing him.

Peek offered up an apologetic smile. 'A few questions about the fire over Chain Street last night. *And* the blood,' he added, after a pause.

'About *what?*' he spluttered innocently, his mind racing as he tried to work out how they'd nailed him so quickly. How the bleeding hell had they managed that? 'Don't know what you're on about,' he said. 'I've been here all night. Since turning out time,' he added hopefully, though he was beginning not to even care.

'Not according to the gentleman who called the fire brigade,' said the other officer. 'Now, are we going to be on our way? It's bloody boracic out here!'

Not *another* bleeding Cockney, Charlie thought. He'd had enough of Cockneys and their back-stabbing ways to last him a lifetime.

But right now, it seemed he was off to the cells. 'Any chance of a wash and something to eat down there?' he asked.

Peek winked at him. 'You know the desk sergeant and how he's a stickler for cleanliness, Charlie. You just offer to give him a cuddle and I'm sure he'll show you where the bathroom is.'

Charlie fell into step with him, feeling strangely weightless. Yes, he decided. Perhaps he would.

It had taken the best part of the morning, and the outcome had been surprising, to say the least. But by the time Charlie was released from nick and strolling back down Toller Lane, the sense of weightlessness had only increased. He had a full belly, had had his wounds dressed and had been able to both have a shave and wash his filthy matted hair. No, all in all, he decided, as he tramped along the glittering pavements, there was a sense of relief about it all.

'Fucking bastards,' Darley said, when Charlie had finally tracked him down. 'Fucking back-stabbing turncoats.'

They were sitting up at the bar in the Unicorn, drinking whiskey and ruminating on the world they'd stumbled into. It was clear as day what had happened and perhaps they should have seen it coming. Perhaps it was always going to happen that the Krays and the Mancs would cut a deal. The Krays were unstoppable and the Mancs probably knew it – but there'd be a price for allowing them to operate on their turf; a cash one, and, given the events of that weekend, a need for honour to be satisfied, of retaliation having to be seen to be done.

And there was no chance they'd ever give up one of their own to the Mancs, was there? No, it suited the Cockneys perfectly to offer up Darley and Charlie; make out they were part of some notorious Bradford gang. Which was laughable really, under the circumstances, Charlie thought. Him in a gang? Never.

All these years Charlie had stood alone, and he always would, too. Oh, yes, many a gang had tried to recruit him, especially back in the days when he was beating people up for fun, for Cappovanni. And especially when he started making such a name for himself on the prize-fighting circuit. But he wasn't recruitable, and nowadays anyone who was anyone (north of the Watford Gap, anyway) knew that Charlie was a gang of one and always would be. Darley had only been roped into this because of his connections with the boxing fraternity and his size.

No. No matter what the southerners thought, or the Mancs for that matter, the only reason the two of them had taken part in any of this was for the money. It was always about the money; Charlie for the here and now, and Darley, who was past his prime as far as training and boxing went, for the cash and the hope that other odd jobs might come his way. Bastard gangsters and their empire building, Charlie thought. He didn't want an empire. He never had before, and he certainly didn't want one now.

What he wanted he couldn't have. Not any more.

The pretty girl behind the pumps had been making eyes at him since they got there, and had already slipped him a couple of whiskies, which made him laugh. He could see his reflection in the mirrored back panel of the bar, and the face looking back at him seemed to belong to someone else. Amazing what a bit of soap from the bathroom in the nick could achieve. He still looked like a bear, but an approachable bear, evidently. Still had whatever it was that his mam always used to say would break a few hearts. He swallowed hard, downed his drink and called her over for another.

'I've admitted arson,' he told Darley. 'Seemed the best thing to do.'

'That's all fucking wrong, mate,' Darley said with feeling. 'Get collared for something you didn't even do?'

Charlie shrugged. 'The brief thought it would make the most sense under the circumstances. They're on to me for the house down on Quaker Lane as well.'

Charlie had his own set of collectors these days. Women he trusted to live in with the prostitutes and run the houses on his behalf. He knew they liked to have a dabble with their favourite punters now and again, but he didn't mind; it was one of the perks as far as he was concerned.

They were good to him and for him, and that was all that mattered. He could go AWOL for weeks or months, and always knew that when he paid a visit – didn't matter if it was for sex or money – there would be a large envelope waiting for him with his cut.

And now it looked like he was going to be AWOL for a good bit, as well.

'Ah,' said Darley, looking gloomily into the new drink that had been put in front of him. 'Sorry to hear that, mate.'

'It was always coming. I've never been quite as good covering my tracks as old Cappovanni, have I?' He grinned at Darley. 'You and me both, eh? No, it's fine,' he said, stretching his back out to ease the stiffness. He was 32, and this morning his body felt it. What he needed was to get himself a few bouts in the ring. Tone him up. Get him back on some sort of track. 'I was lucky to get bail, so he says,' he told Darley. 'They're trying to stick an assault charge on me as well.' He stopped and chuckled. 'Don't see how, though, when the twat who left the blood on the landing is back up Blackpool bloody Tower, lording it over his little kingdom!'

Darley nodded. 'And staying there, as well, if he knows what's good for him. I still can't believe they just offered us up – fucking bastards. Did he say how long you're likely to get?'

Charlie shook his head. It would be weeks before he came to trial – maybe months. He rather wished it would hurry up.

'Oh, just a stretch,' he told his friend.

Chapter 22

November 1955

The weeks, in the end, had turned to months, witnesses willing to testify in court against Charlie having tended to be rather hard to come by. The bastard snow had stopped falling eventually, the freeze had finally thawed and, almost unbelievably, given the suffocating blanket of cold that had lain over the city so long, shoots began pushing through in the beds across the grass from him, and leaves had begun unfurling on the tree.

Now he knew where the immediate future lay, Charlie found a kind of peace. Not contentment – he knew he'd never have the luxury of feeling that again, and nor should he; it wouldn't have seemed right. But at least the knowledge that at some point soon, when they got their bloody skates on and sentenced him, he would have one luxury waiting for him at least. The luxury of not having to think about how to live any more. At least for a bit.

In the meantime, life had gone on just as it had done for the previous two years. The bastard Mancs and Cockney twats had left Bradford alone and he earned enough to get by with his minding and protection, and via the gifts of food and drink people left on his bench. And, as the summer had given way to the chill of early autumn, the odd pullover and blanket as well.

'You're loved, lad,' said Cappovanni, as he pulled on his coat, clapping Charlie affectionately on the shoulder. They'd been sitting in the Boy and Barrel, sharing a quiet afternoon drink for old times' sake. He'd bumped into old Cappovanni earlier, by John St Market, and, with him soon due to be off for a spell at Her Majesty's pleasure, it was an opportune chance for them to catch up.

Although he was knocking on a bit now – somewhere in his seventies, Charlie reckoned – Cappovanni still had his finger in a number of pies. Less business with the prostitutes, yes, because Charlie had all but taken over that side of things, but a lot more on the pawn business side. He'd opened three such shops now and was enjoying semi-retirement – getting other people doing the work for him, just as always. And loyally, too. Old Cappovanni had always fostered that.

Charlie shook his head, feeling embarrassed at his old mentor's sentimentality. That was old age for you. Made you soft. Made you maudlin. It must have, he reflected as the two shook hands on parting and Cappovanni slipped a couple of pounds into his palm.

Still, gift horses and all that, Charlie thought, as he headed off down Ivegate in the direction of his second home, the Unicorn. Cappovanni had apparently seen his brother Reggie heading in there earlier and, knowing Vera would only have let him have enough for a facer, Charlie decided he'd let him have a share in his good fortune.

But as soon as he walked through the door he could see that it wasn't destined to be the companionable couple of drinks he'd imagined. He was finely attuned to the different atmospheres of boozers, and the hairs on his neck had immediately sprung to attention. Something was kicking off.

He scanned the noisy room and noticed how the punters were lowering their eyes as Charlie's gaze came to rest on them. Then he saw what was at the centre of it. *Bleeding Reggie.* There

were two blokes ranting at him, obviously angry about something, and Reggie, cocky as ever, despite being half their size,
was squaring up to the pair of them, obviously trying to goad
them into a fist-fight.

Was he insane? Charlie'd been doing a good job of keeping
out of trouble these last weeks. He'd be sentenced in a few days
and, much as he'd accepted his lot for the immediate future,
there was no sense in making things worse for himself.

But family was family, and, however idiotic his brother was,
he was clearly required to intervene. He strode across the
wooden floor of the pub, the boards creaking under his weight,
with the intention of using nothing but his presence to calm
things down. But it wasn't to be. Vera'd clearly stumped up
some cash because when Reggie looked at him Charlie could
see he was already tight – an assumption he then proceeded to
put beyond reasonable doubt by grinning at his approaching
brother, raising his fist and launching a punch at the chin of
one of the men. *Typical*, Charlie thought, bemused at his brother's stupidity. *He decides to go all bleeding Sugar Ray the minute he
sees me.*

'What's going on, Reggie?' he asked, stepping in front of the
two blokes before either had a chance to retaliate.

'These two bastards!' Reggie spluttered, pointing behind
Charlie. 'Said I pinched one of their bleeding drinks, the
cheeky twats. Never in my bleeding life!' he finished, doing a
good impersonation of someone who was hurt and aggrieved.

Charlie had to stop himself laughing out loud. Maybe Vera
hadn't given him much ale money after all. No, he'd been
helping himself, clearly – minesweeping, as it was called. A
long-time favourite pastime of all the Hudson brothers. You
didn't leave your drinks alone when they were about if you
wanted to find them there when you got back.

Charlie turned around to the two men, who seemed happy to wait for this exchange to happen rather than jumping in and escalating things immediately. Maybe busy figuring out their chances, two on two, now they knew the size of the second opponent. Charlie smiled. No, it wasn't quite two on two, was it? 'If he says he didn't take it,' he told them, 'he didn't take it. Now fuck off!'

The blokes looked to be in their early twenties, one of them built like a brick shit house. And though the other was slightly smaller, both looked like they could handle themselves. A *fair fight, then*, Charlie thought as he mentally prepared himself for some action.

'Buy me another pint then, and we'll leave it,' the bigger of the two said.

Charlie smiled again. 'I won't tell you again, pal,' he warned him. And for a moment it looked like the man might back off. But that wasn't destined to happen either, it seemed, because before Charlie could stop him Reggie picked up an empty glass and smacked it straight into the fellow's head.

The sound of the glass shattering was joined by a low, resigned moan from Ray the landlord, before it *really* kicked off, just as Charlie had expected as soon as the glass found its target. In fact, it turned into mayhem. The two men went down in fairly quick succession, however, and normally Charlie would have left it at that. But there was no stopping Reggie, who was probably trying to make a name for himself, and carried on punching and sticking the boot in till he drew blood and both men were curling up for protection.

But it seemed they weren't quite out for the count. They were young and spirited and clearly not happy at the thought that the gossip would soon be rattling all over Bradford that they'd been royally done over by the Hudsons.

'Hey, Charlie,' the smaller one croaked, 'you fucking shit!'

He was spitting phlegm and blood and had a couple of teeth missing, and with his anger subsiding Charlie's response was to ignore it. But then he spoke again. 'Your Brian?' the lad hissed. 'I went to school with him – you know that? An' I'll tell you what, it's *you* bastards who should be pushing up daisies instead of him, you shit!'

Charlie couldn't have been punched because both men were still groaning on the floor, but he felt his gut give an almighty heave as if he had.

He felt his boot draw back almost automatically. The anger coursed through him like a kind of electricity, which only found its earth when his foot connected with the man's head.

Shaking with anger, he only just stopped himself from doing the same to his brother, for heaping so much crap on his head.

Instead, he spat out a mouthful of blood, walked out of the pub and headed down the street. He didn't look back to see where Reggie was; he didn't want to know. He didn't care. He cared only that he didn't have enough drink inside him to smooth the edges of the anger that still boiled inside him, nor the stomach to drink any either.

No, there was only one thing. Keep walking.

Keith and Annie were in the Lister's Arms on Manchester Road. It was a Friday, which meant his sister had finished work early and, even better, she'd been paid and was happy to treat him to a few drinks, as he was at a loose end. Annie was made up to the nines as usual and looked stunning. All the men in the bar were admiring her, which wound Keith up no end.

Annie was five years his senior, but that didn't stop him feeling protective. She walked in anywhere, any time and, looking like she did, got the attention of every bloke in the room. It had been no different when they were younger and he was knee high to a sparrow, either – he'd batter any bloke who dared try it on with her, not to mention training her up in how to box.

And nothing had changed. She was married to Harry Jagger from across the road now, but she still liked a night out with the lads when she could manage one, and Keith still had to spend a lot of time watching her back.

The juke box was blaring and the pub was already filling up, even though it was still not much past five. Annie leaned close to Keith, having to shout above the din as they waited for their drinks. 'Is that your suit for court?' she asked.

He nodded. It was his only suit, currently.

'Bring it round to mine tomorrow,' she told him, 'and I'll take the sleeves up a bit. Make it look more like it frigging fits you.' She roared with laughter.

'Cheeky mare!' he said, giving her a friendly nudge. 'Our Reggie gave us this, I'll have you know,' he added, straightening and tugging at the lapels. 'Our Vera says it makes me look like Gene Kelly.'

'More like bleeding Grace Kelly!' she shot back, laughing even more. 'Eh,' she added then, as Keith passed her a lemonade – she was up the duff so she was currently off the ale – 'isn't that your mate John over there?'

Keith looked across at the booth Annie was pointing at. He nodded. 'Don't know her, though – that lass with him. Do you?'

She was a pretty girl and she looked much too young to be out drinking. Not to mention much too good for the likes of John Arnold, mate though he was.

But it seemed Annie didn't know who she was either, and she knew everyone. Which made the girl, who had shiny black hair, setting off dazzling white teeth, seem even more appealing somehow. She was pure class. She looked almost like she'd stepped out of a magazine.

'Come on,' he said, drawn by a sudden determination to find out. 'Let's go over and join them, shall we?'

But Annie was already chatting to a bloke who had sidled up, and deciding she was big enough and tough enough to handle him, Keith headed over on his own.

'All right, John?' he said, noticing that the girl was blushing furiously. 'You going to introduce me to your young lady, then?'

John smiled proudly as he stood up to shake Keith's hand. 'Now then, Tucker,' he said, waving an expansive arm towards the girl, 'this is Shirley. Shirley Read. She's from Clayton.'

Ooh, Clayton, Keith thought. He'd never met anyone from Clayton. It was a little village about five miles from Little Horton and he'd thought only posh people lived there. So was *she* posh? She looked posh, for sure. But if that were so, why was she here? What would a posh bird be doing with the likes of John Arnold?

'That's nice,' he answered, for want of anything better to say.

'Yes, and funnily enough,' John said, 'we were just talking about your lot.'

Keith raised his eyebrows. 'We really that interesting, John?' he asked, winking at Shirley. Close up, she really did look very young.

'Well, not your lot exactly,' John corrected. 'Your Charlie. We saw him earlier. On the way here from Shirley's.'

'Charlie?' said Keith, trying to compute the trip from Clayton. 'Whereabouts did you see him?'

'Lidget Green way. Heading towards Legram's Lane. He all right, mate?'

The sound of his brother's name had the usual effect on Keith. What was he up to? How was he doing? *Was* he all right? He'd barely seen him since he'd been charged and had no idea what he was up to. Hardly anyone seemed to these days. But Lidget Green? What would he be doing there? Charlie was a town man. Or, rather, had been – who knew what he might be up to currently? He'd be going down in a couple of weeks now. Maybe he was out and about settling scores or something. But Lidget Green? That made no more sense than would Clayton.

'Who was he with?' he asked John.

John looked slightly uncomfortable. He glanced at Shirley before answering, placing a hand over hers. 'Well, I think he'd been fighting, Keith, to be honest. He was covered in blood, well, his fists were, and his … well, he looked a bit of a mess. And, well, a bit odd.'

'Odd? In what way?'

'Like he was either pissed up or raging at someone, mate. Sorry.'

Keith felt a kind of nausea well in his stomach. If Charlie had been fighting again, it might mean an even longer sentence, and if he had blood on his hands, then, as night followed day, somebody somewhere was hurting.

'You certain it was him, John?' he asked hopefully, already knowing the answer. Everybody knew who Chuck Hudson was. *Everyone*. There was no mistaking him for anyone else.

John duly nodded. And, unsettled by the unwelcome news, Keith knew he needed to get back to Annie. Maybe they should take a bus out there. See if they could find him. In any event, she'd know what best to do.

There was also the small matter of the bloke at the bar. 'Right,' he said. 'Thanks. I'll get back to our Annie and rescue her from Tommy Branning.' He then leaned across to the young girl and held out his hand to her. 'Nice to meet you, Shirley,' he said politely. 'No doubt see you around, eh?'

She blushed engagingly and with something of a glint in her eye, but as Keith headed back to Annie he somehow doubted that very much. God only knew what sort of stuff John had filled her pretty head with about the Hudsons, and he didn't doubt seeing Charlie had finished off anything John had neglected to mention. Pissed up or raging. Neither sounded very good.

'She's from Clayton,' Annie said as Keith joined her again.

'I know.'

'And she's only 15, the bleeding nonce! How old is that lad? Nineteen? Twenty? Shouldn't be allowed.'

'I *know*. Annie, listen. John's just seen our Charlie – staggering around up at frigging Lidget Green somewhere. Covered in blood, by all accounts. What the frig's he doing over there?' He downed the remains of his ale. 'I think we should do something. I think he's probably gone after someone, Annie. And with the sentencing coming up …'

'Or more like already got them,' she corrected. 'If he's covered in blood, I'd say that was the odds-on favourite, wouldn't you?'

Keith conceded that that did make more sense. 'But we should do something, shouldn't we? Go and get our Ronnie, maybe? See if we can find him?'

Annie finished her own drink and placed it on the bar. Being up the duff meant her head was straight at least. She stared thoughtfully ahead for a few seconds before turning and shaking her head.

'I don't think he's gone after someone, anyway,' she eventually said.

'What, then?'

'Well, not like you mean, at any rate.'

'What d'you mean?'

'Well you know what's down Legram's Lane, don't you?'

Keith was getting a little annoyed by his sister trying to be all mysterious, 'No, Annie, I don't,' he said. 'What the frig are you on about? What's down Legram's Lane?'

'The cemetery, you numbskull. He's probably going to the cemetery.'

Keith was shocked. Could that be it? It had never occurred to him. Not because the location of the cemetery had slipped his mind – it hadn't – but because, as far as he knew, Charlie had never set foot in the place since before the accident. Or, if he did, he kept it pretty bloody quiet. No one had seen him there, *ever*; at one time it had been the talk of the whole estate. Why would he go there now? He said as much to Annie.

'God knows,' Annie said, shrugging. 'But if he is, we should leave him to it. It's about bleeding time, in my book.' She grinned at Keith, unconcerned. 'You want another one in there?' she asked him, winking. 'Go on, my little lovebird – my treat.'

Chapter 23

Charlie leaned his back against the dry brick wall that surrounded Scholemoor cemetery, and tried to catch his breath. The anger inside him hadn't diminished on his journey. If anything, it had become more intense.

He hadn't known he was coming here, not when he'd set off. He'd just needed to walk, and this is where his feet had brought him. To the edge of here, anyway. And that was enough for the moment. He let the wall support him, feeling the cold of it seep immediately into him, cooling his skin through the thin wool of his jacket.

There was little left of the day now, and as the sun was going down, so was the temperature. It had been a cold enough one in the first place, bright and sharp, one that seemed to presage another bitter winter. He felt a sudden rush of thanks that he would be spending it inside. And not just to escape the weather, either. He closed his eyes. If only he could escape what was in his head that easily.

'Charlie?'

The unexpected female voice made his eyes snap open. The road had been deserted when he'd shut them. He'd obviously drifted off. But no, he hadn't, he'd just lost himself inside his head for a few moments. Time enough for someone to round the corner.

It was a young blonde woman, her long afternoon shadow falling over him. She was standing in front of him, her hand resting on the handle of a pram.

'It is Charlie, isn't it? Charlie Hudson? You don't remember me, do you?'

He looked up at her, wondering at her boldness in venturing to even speak to him. Aware of the blood crusted over his hands, the splatters on his jacket. Yet she seemed unperturbed.

'You don't, do you?' she added. 'I'm June Holmes. A mate of your Annie's.'

Charlie didn't. Didn't have a clue who she was, but he nodded anyway, even though what he really wanted to do was tell her to piss off and leave him alone. The words came out anyway, as if a part of him didn't want that at all. 'Yeah, course I remember you,' he said, conscious that she was blushing a little. 'Our Annie's mate. Of course. That your nipper?'

He nodded towards the pram and the girl smiled. 'My first,' she said proudly. 'What you doing round here, Charlie?' Her expression changed as she looked past him. 'Oh, of course,' she said softly. Then added, 'Sorry.'

Charlie sucked in another calming breath. The girl seemed lost for words now. 'Well …' she began.

He had a sudden thought. 'You got a cigarette?'

This galvanised her. She rummaged through her bag and found a packet, and when she'd given him one she lit it for him with shaking hands.

'There you go,' she said, seemingly pleased to have been able to do something to help him. It moved him and angered him in equal measure. 'Listen,' she added, placing both hands back on the pram handle. 'I'm sorry about … well, you know. I'm just sorry, all right?'

Charlie took the cigarette and looked down at his feet, 'Right then,' he said. 'You'd best go.' He had a horrible feeling she might want to say something more, and he couldn't have that. He wasn't even sure why he'd asked her for the cigarette – he rarely smoked; could never afford to these days – but right now he felt he needed one and took a long draw as she hurried off down the road.

It was as good as useless, so he bit the tip off and spat it onto the pavement before taking another, stronger draw. It did little to diminish his anger but it did draw his attention to his hands; there was more torn flesh than he'd realised and his knuckles were swelling badly. He must have given those two blokes a right leathering. *Fucking Reggie*, he thought. It had been a fight entirely of his making, and now there was a chance he'd be in more trouble than he already was.

He turned and looked around him. How much trouble was he in really, though, compared to this? This was trouble of a different order. This was trouble that couldn't be crossed off a list once he'd done a few months in the clink. He turned towards the entrance, finally resolute, approaching the enormous iron gates that had always looked like the gates to hell when he was little, and which were thrown wide open to invite people in.

He flicked the cigarette away and placed his bloodied hands in his pockets. Now he was here he was determined to see it through. He walked purposefully onwards into the cemetery proper, ready to face the demons he'd spent so long running away from. *Charlie Hudson*, he thought, with sudden clarity, *who didn't run away from anything or anyone.*

And the running, in the end, had all been pointless. Oh, he'd tried atoning; reasoning that if he let go of all materialistic gains, if he made his life as empty and uncomfortable as he possibly could, if he went cold when others were warm, was angry when others were happy, had nothing when others had plenty – if he did all this, it would represent some kind of penance for what he'd done.

But it wouldn't change anything, would it? It didn't alter the facts.

He sighed as he glanced around the hundreds of graves stretching off into the distance, wondering where the hell to even start. He couldn't even do that much, because he had run away. He'd failed them. And there was nothing he could do that would make up for it. Even admitting to a crime he didn't commit so that he would be sent to jail wasn't sufficient. No, even that – because that, too, was a comfort he didn't deserve; to have the noises of the nick drowning out the demons that had taken up residence in his head and heart.

He continued to walk in the chilly dusk, with no real plan in his head, hoping some sign would manifest itself and help show him the way. And then, rounding a corner of one of the many paths that criss-crossed the cemetery, he stopped in his tracks and blinked. Was that his bleeding *mother*?

Charlie stared. It certainly looked like his mam, and, like the girl earlier, she had a pram with her. He quickened his step. Yes, it was definitely Annie. He recognised her calf-length, turquoise coat. And why wouldn't she be there? The thought seemed to stab at him. One of her sons was buried up here, wasn't he?

Annie was standing in front of a grave, jiggling the pram with one gloved hand, her back towards him, but as he approached some sixth sense must have made her aware of him. She spun round, then, and immediately made the sign of the cross.

'Frigging hell, Charlie!' she gasped, recognising him. 'You frightened me half to death!' She cast her eyes over him. 'What … what are *you* doing here?'

She was looking questioningly into his eyes now and he wasn't sure what to say to her. Instead he looked past her, to the grave in front of her, which was obviously Brian's. He leaned towards the headstone to read the words carved into the stone.

Brian Hudson, he read, *beloved son of Reginald and Annie, a dear brother who will live on in our hearts.*

He read on then, surprised to read that the older brother he'd never known, little Frank, was interred in the same grave. He turned to his mother. 'I don't know, Mam,' he said sadly. 'Just thought I best show me face. You know, before I get sent away.'

Annie's eyes were shining. 'That's a good thing, son. A *good* thing. I wish you weren't going away again,' she added. Then she frowned. 'Aww, son. I'm so sad about everything. But I'm so glad you've come up to see our Brian.' She smiled a wan smile now. 'And our little Frank too, of course.' She turned towards the pram then, and Charlie sensed she was struggling to speak.

'You come up here a lot?' he asked her.

She sniffed. Then smiled as she rocked the pram handle. 'Probably a good bit more that you might think, son. A good bit more than your dad might, an 'all.'

She let go the handle and fished in the pocket of her coat for a hankie. 'I thought I'd bring young Vinnie up,' she said, once she'd blown her nose. 'Give our June a bit of a break. And besides, I thought he should come up and say hello to his uncles. You know babies, Charlie. Sometimes a good walk's all that'll settle them. Might as well walk here as anywhere. I could probably do it with my eyes closed, truth be told.'

Charlie nodded and peeped into the pram. The little boy, not more than a couple of months old yet, opened his eyes, as if on cue, and smiled up at him.

Charlie was choked. But he swallowed it down. 'Is that red hair, Mam?'

Annie laughed as she looked into the pram with him. 'Looks like it, lad, doesn't it? Poor little bugger. Mind you, there were redheads in our family years back, did you know that? Irish, apparently. These things have a habit of popping out when you least expect them.' She glanced up at Charlie. 'Looks like you, though. You know, when you were little.'

'Does he?'

Annie leaned into the pram and picked the baby up with practised ease. 'Here,' she said, passing him out to him. 'Best say hello to him, lad. It might be a long time before you see him again.'

She grinned at his shocked expression, and ignored his protests about the state of his hands. 'Go on, take him,' she said. 'He's all wrapped up. You won't dirty him. Go on. Say hello to him properly while I change these flowers.'

Charlie was mesmerised by how the infant regarded him so steadily. No apparent fear that this big brute had him held in the crook of his arm. He touched Vinnie's cheek, carefully, using the side of his little finger. 'Now then, lad,' he whispered. 'See here, this is where your uncle Brian and uncle Frank are sleeping. Someone'll make sure you hear all about them.'

The baby gurgled and reached out a tiny hand to clasp his finger. Overcome by the intensity of the emotions that were welling up inside him, Charlie lifted the little bundle up to his face and held him close. He leaned into him, instinctively sniffing the soft pink of his tiny head, aware of but no longer caring about the tears that were spilling down his unshaven cheeks. 'I used to have one who smelled just like you, little pal,' he whispered into the baby's ear, before laying him carefully back in his pram before his heart burst out of his chest. He'd not held a baby in so long.

Taking a deep breath that hurt more than any punch to the ribs he'd ever had, he called to his mother, who'd disappeared off to another row of graves. 'Are you ready, Mam?' he called. 'It's getting on a bit. It'll be dark soon. You ought to get the kid back to our June, oughtn't you?'

Annie appeared again, a bunch of dead flowers now in her hand. 'No need to fuss, son,' she said, placing them on the rain cover of the pram. 'I know what the time is. I'm going to walk up to Lidget Green for the bus. And look.' She stopped and pointed to where she'd just been, two rows across. 'Over there, okay, son? You'll soon see it.' She squeezed his arm. 'And listen, when you're done why don't you head back to ours for a bit of tea and a wash and that. I'd like that, you know. And bugger your bleeding dad!'

It was almost fully dark by the time Charlie had watched his mam's progress back out of the cemetery. He wouldn't be going there for any tea, however much he wished he could have told her otherwise. No. He'd be back in the Unicorn and back on his bench, same as always.

He looked across to where his mam had pointed, willing his reluctant feet to move, knowing how hard this was going to be. Perhaps the hardest thing he'd ever done, and maybe that was as it should be. Leaving Brian and Frank's grave, with the pink and white flowers his mama had left still a bright splash of colour against the base of the headstone, he walked the few strides sufficient to get him to the row she'd pointed out.

He saw the grave immediately, by virtue of the same fresh posy of flowers. He didn't know what kind of flowers they were, but they were sat in their jam jar next to another, bigger bunch, which also looked recently placed.

He mouthed the names that were written on the inscription on the headstone. Wondered again about the flowers. Imagined her own mother, and her father too, coming here often, just as his mam did, separate but united by the same grief he had caused. He thought of the baby he'd just held and the baby he would never hold again; of the wife he had promised he would cherish for all time. The wife he'd told her father he would lay down his life for. He felt a sob forming in his throat. It was so wrong. It should have been *his* life that had been lost. Not hers. Not *theirs*.

He dropped to his knees then, the need to be closer to the woman and child he'd loved suddenly urgent and compelling. And as he knelt on the pebbled surface of the grave, he noticed that in front of the jam jar was propped a handwritten note. He stretched forward to pick the card up.

Rest in peace my darlings, his mother had written. *We all miss you dearly, especially Charlie, your beloved husband and daddy.*

Charlie clutched the note to his chest and raised his eyes to the heavens. 'Why?' he raged to the God who'd decided to punish him for all eternity. 'Why?'

Then he lay down full length on the grave and finally wept.

Chapter 24

22 December 1955

Keith scowled at his reflection in the mantelpiece mirror in the back room. This was no way to be spending his 18th birthday. He should be looking forward to a day of drink and mayhem with his mates, but instead he'd had to get up ridiculously early, be donned in his suit at nine o'clock in the morning, and trying to flatten his sodding frigging curls with a comb and a cup of sugar water.

'Great birthday this is going to be!' he grumbled as he gave up on his hair and threw the comb onto the mantelpiece in a temper. 'I wouldn't mind, but our Charlie won't give a frig whether we're there or not. And why does it have to be me goes down there with you anyway?'

'Shut it, Keith,' his mam snapped. 'I've already told you. You're coming with me and there's an end to it.' She narrowed her eyes at him. 'You, out of all of them, know how important this is. If that bleeding waste of a space father won't come and support his eldest son in court, we *have* to. And before you ask,' she added, 'why else d'you think, you idiot? Look around you. All the others are at frigging work, that's why!'

Keith had a joke he'd always cracked on his birthday, which was something of a family tradition by now. He'd joke that if only Annie hadn't been so eager to push him out and be shut of him, he might have shared the crown with the great man himself. No jokes today, though. Today he'd be stuck down the courts, having to spend hours hanging around and listening to his brother get sentenced to a stretch. And knowing Bradford courts, he would probably be stuck there all day, missing out on some serious partying with the boys.

It wasn't about presents. They didn't swap presents. There were just too many of them. But a birthday – he felt his shoulders droop; it would be a whole year till the next one – meant missing a whole day and night on the town. It was a tragedy, that's what it was.

But he could see from his mam's face that she was really anxious. 'All right, Mam,' he grudgingly reassured her, 'keep your hair on. Though I don't know what you're fretting about – you know what's going to happen. Our Charlie knows he's going down, and *he's* not bothered.'

Annie was adjusting her best blue hat in the mirror. She'd spent 15 minutes choosing it over the other one she'd brought down, because it almost matched her coat, but not quite. As if anyone even cared, thought Keith. She looked at his reflection in the mirror. 'That's exactly *why* I'm worried, lad,' she told him. 'He *should* be bleeding bothered. It's not natural to *want* to go to bleeding jail, is it?'

Keith shrugged. As far as he was concerned, Charlie was better off in prison. Three meals a day, a nice comfy bed and mates to talk to. For someone like Charlie, what wasn't there to like about all that? He kept this piece of wisdom to himself, however, quite sure that his mam would disagree, and instead grabbed the comb again and had another go at taming his hair. She was obviously going to be fiddling about for ages.

Hat and hair details sorted, they arrived at the court building on Manor Row at ten o'clock sharp, having travelled there on the half past nine bus to town. To Keith's delight, they were immediately ushered into courtroom number 2. Maybe this wasn't going to take as long as he thought.

It wasn't often that a case got heard so early in the morning. From what he remembered about their Malcolm's many appearances in court, you could wait ages before you were seen. Mind you, Keith reminded himself, this *was* just a sentencing. The trial had already been heard and Charlie found guilty. Perhaps these kinds of hearings were a lot quicker; after all, the judge had probably decided on the sentence ages ago, truth be told. It lifted his mood as he strutted into the large, airy room. Party time might conceivably still be on the cards then, and at least he was already dressed for the occasion.

He sat down with his mam at the end of a huge bench and took his first proper look around the court. Charlie had yet to be brought to the stand, and Keith wondered what it must have been like to be his brother that morning, waking up and getting dressed – well, perhaps, in Charlie's case, already dressed – and heading off to the courthouse to stand in the dock knowing you were going to be handcuffed and taken away to prison.

Was there any part of him wondering if he should make a run for it? He supposed not, or else they would never have given him bail. No, Keith was clear. Charlie didn't mind going to prison. He wasn't just saying it to impress.

The judge wasn't in either but, looking all around him, Keith could see the benches filling up with loads of people that they knew. Not just Charlie's men, past and present – though there were loads and loads of them – but almost all his own mates, as well. He was genuinely puzzled, not to mention delighted, to see them there. Titch Williams and his older brother, Eddie Lowther and Brian Jarvis, even John Arnold and his pretty little bird, Shirley. He watched her take her seat, carefully smoothing her skirt under her bottom as she sat down. And was she looking at him and blushing again, or was he imagining it? There were also the Herson lads, the McArthurs, the Binns – so many people. The more he looked the more he realised that the courtroom was getting packed. It looked like half the frigging estate had turned out to see Charlie off; men and women, fighters and toe rags; the whole kit and caboodle. Bar Tommy Butler, of course.

'Have you *seen* all these, Mam?' Keith whispered to Annie incredulously. 'Everyone we know – *everyone* – is here.'

Annie nodded. 'I know, lad. And that's because they all respect our Charlie,' she added proudly. She placed a hand on his arm then. 'But you know what the saddest thing is?' Keith shook his head. 'That Charlie probably won't see it like that. He'll just think they've come down just to see him get his just deserts. But they haven't, you know. They've come to show respect.'

Keith was truly astounded at this news. He knew people were *scared* of Charlie, because everyone was. But they also respected him? He hadn't realised that at all. But perhaps he wouldn't have. To Keith he would always just be Charlie. The big brother who taught him how to box and, where necessary, clipped him round the ear, and who, of late, had, well … become not like Charlie any more.

A door at the front opened then and everyone strained to look as Charlie was brought to the stand. Keith was open-mouthed. In a smart suit, clean-shaven and with his wild black hair tamed, Keith hardly recognised his brother. And as he watched him, he started seeing him in a different light. Charlie was a powerful man, and his mam was obviously right – people did respect him. They must do, you could tell by their faces. Keith had been to court with friends on countless occasions and he had *never* seen a turnout like this.

The sentencing was quick – even quicker than he could have imagined. The judge read out the details of the charges that Charlie had pleaded guilty to, and then finished on the words they'd all come here to hear: 'I hereby sentence you to serve 12 months in prison.'

The gavel banged down then and Keith watched Charlie avidly, trying to gauge what his response to that might be. But Charlie looked transfixed, like he wasn't even hearing the words spoken, his gaze steady now, behind Keith, on the back of the court.

Keith swivelled to see for himself what Charlie was looking at. And as he did so, he almost fell backwards. What Charlie was looking at was Reggie, their dad, who was now standing at the back by the door. He was looking straight back at Charlie, and as the silence in the court lengthened so, slowly, did everyone else in the court do as Keith had just done – follow Charlie's gaze and watch the stand-off between the two men.

Charlie had looked shocked at first, but now his expression had hardened. His lips had twisted into a familiar fighting snarl and, not taking his eyes off his dad for a moment, he lowered his face slightly and spat onto the floor, as if trying to psych out an opponent.

It was the move his two police guards had been waiting for. They grabbed him firmly by the arms and started to try to get him out of the booth to take him down the dreaded steps to the cells.

Keith braced himself, ready for the action that might be coming. What were they thinking? Two coppers to try and restrain his huge lump of a brother? They must need their heads testing. Would Charlie now try to throw in one last fight for good measure? It would be a while now before he had his liberty back, after all. But it seemed Charlie had something rather different in mind, something that, even as it began, Keith knew would stay in people's minds for ever. Charlie threw his head back, and to the shock of everyone, started singing.

Ohhhh,
We are the Canterbury Warriors
We stay out late at night
If anybody dare come near us
There's sure to be a fight …

Keith couldn't believe what he was witnessing. The two policemen looked across to the judge, who seemed every bit as bemused as they were, as they continued to try and move Charlie down from the dock. 'Try' being the operative word; everybody watching already knew that. Charlie would only move when he wanted to. And he didn't seem to want to move quite yet.

And it seemed nobody else wanted Charlie to move either. Because, as Charlie took a breath in to start the second verse, he was no longer singing on his own. It started quietly, but then it grew louder and louder, as more voices joined in with Bradford's most famous song, Keith and Annie included.

Last night we were in trouble
Tonight we are in jail
We're doing six months hard labour
For pulling a donkey's tail
Way back whoa back
Come and get yer money back …

The courtroom was really in full swing now. Feet were stamping and fists were being banged onto benches, and despite the judge's call for order and the pounding of his gavel, the song continued, destined to be sung.

> Pea and pies for supper
> Our old lass has plenty of brass
> And we don't give a bugger!

The cheer that went up at the end made the light fittings rattle, and as feet stamped in unison and hands banged together, Keith watched his brother perform his grand finale. With a mighty roar, he forced his arms away from the stunned policemen, and raised them, still cuffed, above his head. He knew, Keith decided. His mam had been wrong. Charlie knew the people here were on his side.

And Keith was glad. He was certainly cheering the hardest as Charlie took one last look around at his friends, let his eyes dwell for just a moment on his father, but then move swiftly on, before bowing extravagantly from the waist to the court; first to the left, then to the right and, finally, and very grandly, to the centre.

'Okay then, lads,' he said to his guards, 'time to go home.'

Even then, people seemed reluctant to leave. The applause continued to ring out long after Charlie was finally taken down, and the next time Keith looked around for a sight of his father he had disappeared.

His friends hadn't, however, and when he and Annie finally emerged onto the street, they were all gathered outside, ready for their day and night on the town, energised by the spectacle of the scene they'd just witnessed, and with the Canterbury Warriors chant still ringing in their ears.

Keith raised his fists above his head joyously, grinning from ear to ear. 'What a fucking birthday!' he said to Titch Williams.

Epilogue

Charlie Hudson, Chuck or Tucker. However anyone remembers Charlie, it is usually with great respect, and always with an accompanying story of something they saw him do, or something they'd heard about him. Charlie lived through four generations of the Hudson family before he finally met his maker. By the time he died, he had already long lost the will to live. He yearned for the kind of peace that only the long sleep could bring.

Keith, the only remaining sibling now, remembers Charlie as being an indomitable force right to the end, though he says that in his later years Charlie could be a pain in the arse. Though he slept alone on his bench almost until the end, Keith and his wife Shirley took care of him whenever they could. Not that Charlie liked it – even when he was in his late sixties he would threaten to knock Keith out if he didn't leave him be.

Some Charlie facts: He never burgled anybody. He never disrespected the elderly. He never used bad language around women or when in polite company. Despite the tragedy of his early life, in his latter years he was always up for a laugh. He was fiercely loyal to those he cared about. That so many people loved him didn't happen by accident.

Personally, I remember my uncle Charlie only as an old man, although he was only in his forties when I was born. But still as a fighter and always as a loner, his heart having been broken so comprehensively so long before. During the 1970s, sons of old enemies would go looking for Charlie to avenge an old grudge for their fathers. Everyone knew where to find him. Through the day he'd be sitting at 'his' table in either the Unicorn or Yates's, his enormous fists on the table in front of him, flexing and unflexing, ready and waiting for anything that might come his way. When confronted, Charlie didn't usually speak. He didn't need to. Would simply roll up his sleeves or take off his overcoat and slam his aggressor to the ground with one smack. No one ever recalls Charlie having to buy a drink for himself in his later years. He never had to.

My own children, Kylie and Scott, also remember their great uncle Charlie with great fondness. As small children, they lived in the town-centre pub I used to run, the Washington, which was just opposite Charlie's bench. All the other kids were afraid of the giant man who slept outside with his wild, white hair and matching bushy beard. Not Kylie and Scott. To them he was the image of Father Christmas, and they loved to be allowed to run over to him and plant a few pounds in his hand. They never noticed how he stared at them, not knowing who they were.

Rest in peace, Uncle Charlie.

Julie Shaw, October 2014

Glossary

Facer or facer inner/seer inner – enough money to buy your first drink.

Spice – sweets.

Nashing – getting out of there. Fast.

Muck hook – woman of loose morals. A slapper.

Acknowledgements

I would like to thank my agent Andrew Lownie for this wonderful opportunity to tell my stories, and the team at HarperCollins for putting their trust in me every step of the way. I also want to thank the wonderful Lynne Barrett-Lee for helping me turn my dream into reality. Without her help, these stories would still be in the box in my garage, gathering dust.

I would like to dedicate these books first and foremost to my parents Keith and Shirley Hudson. They made me who I am today, and have loved and supported me all my life. And to my gorgeous husband Ben, who has had to endure me practically ignoring him for two years while I worked on my writing, and who learned how to cook, clean and work the washing machine while I was in my 'zone'. I also need to mention my brother Glenn and sister Paula, who have giggled along with me as I decided what material to use and what most definitely needed to stay buried, and my cousin Susan Taylor (our Nipper), who has been on hand whenever I needed her for historical accuracy or juicy snippets. All of my family deserve a mention, but they are legion and mentioning them all would fill a book. They know how much I love them.

Finally, I also dedicate all these words to my favourite ever cousin, Willie Jagger. Rest in peace, Willie. You know how much you're loved and no doubt you'll be laughing your arse off up there at the thought of me being an author. Every time I see our Pauline it makes me so happy because she reminds me of everything you were.

12290149R00143

Printed in Germany
by Amazon Distribution
GmbH, Leipzig